Diversity, Resiliency, Legacy

✦

The Lives of Adult Students at Tufts University

Jean Herbert and Tina Marie Johnson

iUniverse, Inc.
New York   Bloomington

Diversity, Resiliency, Legacy

The Lives of Adult Students at Tufts University

Copyright © 2008 by Jean Herbert and Tina Marie Johnson

All rights reserved. No part of this book may be used or reproduced by any means, graphic, electronic, or mechanical, including photocopying, recording, taping or by any information storage retrieval system without the written permission of the publisher except in the case of brief quotations embodied in critical articles and reviews.

iUniverse books may be ordered through booksellers or by contacting:

iUniverse
1663 Liberty Drive
Bloomington, IN 47403
www.iuniverse.com
1-800-Authors (1-800-288-4677)

Because of the dynamic nature of the Internet, any Web addresses or links contained in this book may have changed since publication and may no longer be valid. The views expressed in this work are solely those of the author and do not necessarily reflect the views of the publisher, and the publisher hereby disclaims any responsibility for them.

ISBN: 978-0-595-50046-8 (pbk)
ISBN: 978-0-595-61354-0 (ebk)

Printed in the United States of America

iUniverse rev. date: 7/29/09

Acknowledgements

We gratefully acknowledge the hard work and patience of the following people:

Lead Researchers: Jean Herbert, Tina Marie Johnson
Lead Research Assistant: Katerina Lucas
Research Assistants: Derek Benoit, Janet Wilkins
Cover Art Photographer: Clark E. Duverger

This project could not have been completed without
the financial support and encouragement from the following:

Jonathan M. Tisch College of Citizenship and Public Service at Tufts University

The Arts & Sciences and Engineering Diversity Fund of Tufts University

Office of the Dean of Undergraduate Education

The Pratt Family

The Bernard Osher Foundation

The Returning Students Organization

The Tufts Community Union

President Lawrence S Bacow
We would like to thank all the students, faculty, and staff who participated in and supported this project and the R.E.A.L. Program. We would also like to thank the Tufts administration for their commitment to providing a quality education to an under-served population.

Table of Contents

Acknowledgements...v

Preface ix

Foreword xi

Introduction...xiii

Diversity... *1*

    Edwin Ortiz 3

    Benjamin Presnell..11

    Katerina Lucas...15

    Nathan Alden...21

    Tyler Dennison 25

    Joanne Walker 29

    Bernard Zirnheld..33

    Ruth...37

    Delis Etienne...41

    Kathryn Sutton 43

    Jane Wahome 45

    Ofir Braverman 47

    Hiro Nakajima 49

    Eri Takashima..51

    Tobias Bonthrone 53

    Scott Arsenault..57

    Bonnie Chou..61

    David Kuo 63

Resiliency... *65*

    Edita Zlatic 67

    Sue Meaney 71

    Derek Benoit 79

    Theresa Maggiore 85

    Michelle Botus 87

    Laura M. 89

George 95

Amy (Scallon) Adolfo 99

Sarah Mocas 103

Eric Erkenbrack 105

Peter Malkin...107

Stephanie Tusa...111

Marilyn Glazer-Weiser..113

Legacy *115*

Tina Johnson...117

Soledad Montanes-Ordovas..123

Delores Huff 127

Richard May 129

Luis Martinez 133

Erika Sonder 135

William...137

Charles Paulding 141

Gitta Rohweder..145

Thomas Payne 149

Marcey Marold...153

Friends of the R.E.A.L. Program *155*

Bobbie Knable..157

Marian Connor 159

Frederick and Eleanor Pratt 163

Rocco Carzo 167

John Hammock 173

Molly Mead..177

Robert Fera 181

Robert Hollister 185

Barbara Rubel...189

Preface

JEAN HERBERT, Director of the R.E.A.L. Program

Nearly 400 adult students have graduated from Tufts University since 1970. In this book you will learn about their experiences as non-traditional students at a selective university through interviews and essays. In creating this book, we explored the impact of the R.E.A.L. program on Tufts as well as on the lives of the students. We found three major points of impact: diversity, resiliency, and legacy.

In each section of the book you will read about students from diverse backgrounds who overcame many obstacles to succeed at Tufts. Many of them have created a legacy, not only by what they accomplished at Tufts, but also by inspiring others in their families to further their education.

When Russell E. Miller published his history of Tufts University to commemorate its centennial, his purpose was informed by his role as university archivist as well as by his position as a professor of history. Volume I recorded the development of Tufts from its beginning as a small Universalist institution, established in 1852 primarily to educate future clergymen, to its emergence as a respected co-educational liberal arts college. Volume II, published in 1986, continued this historical format, covering the years 1952 to 1983.

When Sol Gittleman, provost of Tufts for 21 years, wrote <u>An Entrepreneurial University: The Transformation of Tufts University</u>, he defined his purpose as chronicling "an institutional metamorphosis at a time of remarkable change in this country's understanding of the university and its culture." As the title implies, this book relates--in part--the financial challenges faced by Tufts as it grew into an internationally recognized university, acting on its vision often before resources were fully available.

Professor Gittleman's book is about people, the top-level administrators who made the decisions and effected the changes that made Tufts what it is today. Our book is also about people, but it is about the students whose lives were radically changed by the education they received at Tufts University in the small program designed for adults that began in 1970.

With funding from the Tisch College of Citizenship and Public Service as well as the Tufts Diversity Fund, we interviewed alumni and current students in the R.E.A.L. Program (Resumed Education for Adult Learners). We also asked faculty members and administrators to share their impressions of what the adult students had brought to Tufts. The compilation of these interviews and essays creates one more piece to add to the historical record of Tufts, this time from the unique perspective of the students themselves.

We have divided the book into four sections. The first describes the diversity that these students have brought to the Tufts student body, not only through their age and life experience but also through the economic diversity they bring. In addition, of course, they come from different racial, ethnic, and religious backgrounds, with different sexual orientations and abilities.

In the second section we hear from students who faced particular challenges in their efforts to complete their undergraduate education: several women who survived cancer, a man who overcame addiction, a mother whose son was born blind and deaf.

The third section relates the legacy created by this opportunity provided by Tufts. One woman carried her baby across the stage at her graduation; seventeen years later her son entered Tufts as a traditional-age freshman in Fall 2007. Another woman who had been homeless with her four children has broken the cycle of domestic violence that led to her homelessness.

In the fourth section we hear from people outside the program who have understood the importance of providing a quality education to these unique students. Mr. and Mrs. Pratt explain how they came to provide a scholarship and other funding for the program in memory of their daughter Theresa. Tufts faculty, staff, and administrators describe their interactions with some of the adult students. Several people mention the importance of the kind of leadership President Bacow has provided in support of Tufts' mission in opening its doors to these non-traditional learners.

Russell Miller dedicated seven pages of his book to describing the inception and early years of the adult student program. Since then the profile of the adult students entering Tufts has changed. But the three themes of diversity, resiliency, and legacy have remained consistent. Our book illustrates through student narratives the diversity the adults from different backgrounds have brought to Tufts, the resiliency they have demonstrated in overcoming tremendous obstacles to obtain an education, and the legacy that their accomplishment has provided to themselves, to their families, and to the university.

Foreword

SOL GITTLEMAN, University Professor and former Provost at Tufts University

One of the endearing and quirky characteristics of Tufts over the years has been a willingness to dive into innovation without financial resources, simply because it was, at the time, the "right" thing to do.

For example, nearly forty years ago, two Tufts Medical School professors, Jack Geiger and Count Gibson, proposed that our impoverished Medical School should provide health care for the Columbia Point Housing Project in Boston. They had a vision of a community health care center providing poor people with a quality of health service that did not exist anywhere in the country; and it came to pass. Every community health care center in the country owes its existence to the efforts of these two Tufts physicians.

In 1964, a few years before the explosion of campus unrest tore into the curriculum of American colleges and universities, a few Tufts faculty members, with the approval of President Nils Wessell, created the Experimental College. The idea of student-led seminars and community-based teachers without the usual credentials was over the edge. There were no other experimental colleges in the country at the time. Tufts again stretched its resources to make this happen.

By the later 1960s, Tufts again led the way, this time by providing a quality education to adult women who had seen their education interrupted. When Antonia Chayes became Dean of Jackson College in 1968, she arrived with a powerful idea. She created a program that would admit qualified women as regular undergraduates, institute a family life center where these women could gather to learn about social issues to help them succeed, and begin a child care center for these women and the surrounding community. All of these goals were achieved.

The first group of ten students in the Continuing Education Program entered Tufts in 1970. Four of them had previous college experience; the other six had none. They all had lots of desire and will. They ranged in age from 29 to 50. Some had children, some did not. With its meager resources, Tufts provided financial aid in the form of grants instead of just loans.

From the outset there was a special symbiosis between the traditional-aged undergraduate women and these late learners. The women's movement on campus, the inchoate Women's Studies Program, drew its inspiration from these older students and their association with the younger female undergraduates.

It was inevitable that men, particularly veterans returning from the Vietnam War, took a look and saw the opportunity. The Seven Sisters women's colleges had also begun welcoming back older female students. But Tufts was co-educational and could do more. In 1976, Tufts began admitting men to the program. In 1983, the program was re-named Resumed Education for Adult Learners.

For those of us who have taught classes with these adult learners, we know the benefit of having people who are closer in age to the instructor. There is a shared historical memory that enriches the experience for the entire class. Some of my R.E.A.L. students have gone on to medical, dental, and veterinary schools; some have won Fulbrights. At least one is a professional musician.

Two presidential wives took a special interest. Betty Mayer, who had completed her undergraduate degree at the Harvard Extension School when she was in her fifties, embraced the R.E.A.L. students at Tufts; and Nancy DiBiaggio, a working woman all her life, found inspiration in these adult learners and went back to school during her years at Tufts. She eventually went on to a graduate program at the Fletcher School.

Whatever the future holds, Tufts was there when we were needed for these older students. We made a difference, and we still can.

Introduction

MINDY NIERENBERG, Student Programs Manager, Tisch College of Citizenship and Public Service

The mission of the Jonathan M. Tisch College of Citizenship and Public Service is "*to prepare Tufts students to become engaged public citizens and community leaders who will help build a more equitable world.*" Why, therefore, did Tisch College choose to collaborate with the R.E.A.L. Program to create this book? The answer may not be immediately obvious, yet the connections are there. In my mind, this nexus lives under the surface as a root system that feeds the Tufts University vision, and serves to support the institution as a thriving, vibrant community.

What does it mean to be an *engaged public citizen*? At Tisch College we define it as "understanding and believing in the democratic ideals of participation and the need to incorporate the voice, perspective, and contributions of every member of the community." The R.E.A.L. program was founded to offer a chance for an education to adult women who did not previously have access to a selective university, women who through familial responsibilities or societal norms were restricted from pursuing knowledge, contributing to the community and having their voices be heard. Since that first day in 1970 when women became the first R.E.A.L. students, and then since 1976 when the program began to include adult men, the R.E.A.L. program has provided otherwise disenfranchised or adult learners the powerful tool of a Tufts education. The R.E.A.L. program itself is *helping to build a more equitable world* by virtue of its very existence.

Many R.E.A.L. students come to Tufts as "engaged public citizens." They have done active citizenship work in their home communities, or in some cases on a national or international level. While at Tufts, many of these

R.E.A.L. students are able to leverage their previous experiences to new levels of engagement, benefiting not only those communities they work with, but the Tufts population as well.

Michelle Botus attended Bunker Hill Community College as a formerly homeless single mother, supported by the One Family Scholars Program, "a not-for-profit organization devoted to ending family homelessness in Massachusetts." Michelle successfully earned her associate's degree from Bunker Hill, where she gave back to that community consistently through her work in student government and as the student member of the school's Board of Trustees. At Tufts, she received a Civic Engagement Fund grant from Tisch College for her work with Project Hope, a nonprofit based in Dorchester that "works in partnership with families so they can move up and out of poverty." She assists adult learners prepare for the GED by providing women with one-on-one tutoring.

Last year, a team of students in the Media and Public Service course "Producing Films for Social Change" created a film featuring Michelle called "The Price of Education." The film focused on Michelle's resiliency, her goal to be educated, and her work to conquer poverty for her own family and others. It was a revelation to many 'traditional-aged' students that R.E.A.L. students such as Michelle are fellow classmates, and have overcome incredible odds to be here. Over two hundred attended the showing of that film; countless more have viewed the DVD or seen it on the program's website and benefited from its message.

Tina Johnson, the Tufts doctoral student leading the creation of this book, was a R.E.A.L. student as a Tufts undergraduate. Tina came to Tufts through the encouragement of a faculty member at the community college Tina attended in Virginia. She grew up living at times in poverty with her single mother and siblings, and had never dreamed about the possibility of attending a school like Tufts. In rural Virginia, Tina did community-based work, running an after-school program and working with juveniles who had been sentenced to community service. Tina graduated from Tufts, stayed to get her Master's in Child Development, and is now in the Interdisciplinary Ph.D. Program.

Tina has been a role model not only for Tufts students but for others, including her own mother. Tina's mother had been in and out of prison over the years. Inspired by her daughter, she began teaching fellow incarcerated women to read, and when released from prison went to college to become a social worker. For the past two and a half years, Tina has been a work-study assistant at Tisch College, advising Citizenship and Public Service Scholars and serving as the graduate assistant for the Active Citizenship Summer

Program. Students have benefited greatly from Tina's perspectives and the depth of knowledge and compassion that she brings to her work.

The junction of the R.E.A.L. program, Tisch College, and Tufts University is one of reciprocity and mutual benefits. The R.E.A.L. students bring perspectives to both the classroom and co-curricular life that would otherwise be absent. The Tufts University vision statement reads: "We value a diverse community of women and men of different races, religions, geographic origins, socioeconomic backgrounds, sexual orientations, personal characteristics, and interests--where differences are understood and respected." The R.E.A.L. program brings to Tufts all of these factors, yet it brings another diversity criterion not stated, that of age and experience. R.E.A.L. students, through virtue of their previous life experiences, contribute to a dynamic, vital center of learning. Gender equity, socioeconomic class, immigration, and countless other issues lie within the lives of R.E.A.L. students, who bring these rich perspectives to the Tufts campus.

"As an institution, we are committed to improving the human condition through education and discovery. Beyond this commitment, we will strive to be a model for society at large. We want to foster an attitude of 'giving back,' an understanding that active citizen participation is essential to freedom and democracy, and a desire to make the world a better place." This, too, is a part of the Tufts vision statement. Its connection to Tisch College is readily apparent, yet when one views this vision through the lens of the R.E.A.L. program, the intersection gains another dimension. The existence of the R.E.A.L. program is a demonstration of this commitment on an institutional level. There is recognition that there are members of society whose 'human condition' has prevented access to higher education at a time in the life cycle when those more privileged are able to attend college. The R.E.A.L. program allows men and women access to education that would otherwise not be possible.

Dean Robert Hollister, a founder and Dean of Tisch College, has written: "lives of active citizenship are not a string of episodic acts; rather they are a journey, a life-long exploration and quest, a lifelong process of trying out new approaches, and of rethinking and learning." Learning, too, is a lifelong process. We cannot fully measure the effects that Tufts has had on R.E.A.L. students, nor the effects of the R.E.A.L. program on Tufts. Yet this book attempts to do just that, and between its pages lie real stories of real people who have achieved what many have considered the impossible. They have a Tufts education and Tufts itself, through the creation and sustenance of the R.E.A.L. program, has demonstrated its commitment to "building a more equitable world."

Diversity

The R.E.A.L. program provides opportunities for those students who have had to overcome a wide array of societal roadblocks in order to arrive at a four-year, selective institution. These include socio-economic obstacles, obstacles pertaining to physical and mental disabilities, and perhaps those obstacles more hidden and entrenched in our society related to race, gender, and religion.

Edwin Ortiz

Q: Please describe to me a regular day in your life before you decided to go back to college.

A: I was the associate director at a public access television station. That meant being in charge of the daily operations at that station. We taught classes in video production and I also produced some television shows at the station.

Q: What was it that made you go back to college?

A: I had previously started a degree in music at Berklee School of Music. At some point in this process I decided that I didn't want to be a performer anymore and I got this arts administration job, which led to my job at the television station. So, here I was in this position as an associate director without a degree. And, well, while I knew that the work I was doing was good, I always wondered what was missing. What information didn't I have that my colleagues with degrees did have? I guess I had a private chip on my shoulder about a private insecurity about what I didn't know.

Q: So, you decided that you had to go back to school. How did you go about that?

A: At first I did not know if I would be able to do it. I was a little insecure about it. And I thought what I would do was to set goals for myself and accomplish them. A long-term goal for me at the time was to run the Boston Marathon. Which seems like it has nothing to do with going back to school,

3

but for me it was a crucial part. What I needed was a record of success for myself, a long-term goal that I could point to. To run the Boston Marathon you have to first qualify by running a previous marathon. You have to train, run and qualify for that marathon and then you have to qualify for the Boston Marathon.

I joined a running club; and I trained with them, and I said this is my goal and I have never run like this before. I've done a little bit of running, a bit of jogging, but I was not an athlete. I've never joined that part of school; you know, I did the arts. So, I trained with this club. I said my goal is to qualify. Is this crazy? And they said: "Well, it is unusual but it is not crazy, it is possible." And that is all I needed, and I trained like crazy, I followed their advice, I followed a program. And I qualified for my first marathon. Then I ran the Boston Marathon. I finished it in a little over three hours. That was important because that whole process took a year and I knew that going back to school was not a short-term thing either. It wasn't simply taking a class; it was to represent a lifestyle change for me.

So, I had coffee with my executive director one January, and I said: "In a year's time I will be leaving this organization and going to school full time." Around this time also, I started to take a night course at U Mass. The next semester I took a class at the Harvard Extension School, and the next semester I took another, to warm up for what I was about to do.

I started to look for programs for adults, but again I realized that I wanted the full-time experience. One program I looked at was at Lesley, which seemed very, very good for adults, but it wasn't a traditional experience by any means. And that is what was most appealing about Tufts. I could register with traditional aged college students but still had the support of the R.E.A.L. program to walk me through this. And when I got accepted, I was thrilled, absolutely thrilled.

Q: How did your friends, your family feel about your decision to go back to school?

A: For the most part, everybody was incredibly supportive. Some people were surprised and impressed that I was going back full time. Like, how was I going to do that financially? You know what a life style change that was going to be. I have to say that my partner was very inspirational in the process. When I first started to look at programs to go back to school, I was looking at schools that were less challenging than Tufts and he told me: "You are smarter than that." And that was what inspired me even to apply to Tufts because I really hadn't formed that part of my consciousness that I could go to a school as good and as challenging and as reputable as Tufts. So it was somebody close to me who was saying you can do this. And, he was really supportive. My family was supportive. My parents were a little confused about my quitting the job to do it, but they were happy I went back to school.

Q: How was your first semester at Tufts? For every student the first semester is a little different and we all come with expectations. Some get fulfilled, some don't.

A: My expectations were absolutely fulfilled. I was completely ready, but it was really challenging. Having the R.E.A.L. program seminar was important. Although I had been taking classes, you know, taking three classes at a time was new. I actually worked my first semester. I worked two part-time jobs at first. I stayed as a bookkeeper at the television station and I became a bookkeeper for another organization. These places were very flexible with me, but it was challenging to be working and going to school at the same time.

Q: How would you describe your interaction with the regular undergraduate students?

A: It was great. I think that they were surprised by having someone a little bit older in the class. But I think that a lot of them, like working in group projects for example, they appreciated my work experience, my real world experience that I brought to things. I think their struggles at their age, at their stage of development, allowed me to be in touch with a different generation in a way that I wasn't necessarily in touch with. So, I think it was mutually beneficial. I have to say though that even though I am a night person, but undergrads are really night people and sometimes that was a little bit of a challenge. I was typically not working on my homework past 1 am. There were a couple of times I pulled an all-nighter, but very rarely. And the undergrad group, you know, they would just say, "Let's get together at 11, how does that sound?" And I would say, "OK, but you have me for exactly 2 hours."

Q: I know you studied abroad. Where did you go?

A: I studied in Madrid for the whole year. It was incredible. I had never been to Europe before and this is an incredible opportunity. I was able to visit the major cities in Western Europe and I got to learn a lot about Spain. I can't say one bad thing about the Tufts in Madrid program. It's so well done. Every

6   Diversity, Resiliency, Legacy

detail has been worked out. They cut through the Spanish bureaucracy before you even get there. And it is a completely educational experience. And all the excursions have been very well thought out with experts telling you about the significance of everything you are seeing. It was an amazing learning opportunity. It changed the way I saw the world, it opened an opportunity for me, because actually as a result of having studied in Spain that year, I was able to go back the year after graduation as a Fulbright Scholar.

Q: Was it hard for you to decide to go to Spain? Because when I think about myself, I suppose I would think about leaving my friends and family behind, to go for a year to a program which is created for people who are around 20 years old.

A: I think what you just asked were two different things. Leaving your family and friends for a year is one part, and then another part is about the way the program is designed. I will say that the program is designed so that anybody would benefit from it. The other part. That was a big decision. My partner and I decided that this was a once in a lifetime opportunity. And in terms of leaving my friends, I have to be honest, with me going back to school, lots of my friendships were kind of on hold anyway because of the demanding schedule of being an undergrad at Tufts. And in some ways, that was a little bit less tough. But it was the absolutely right decision for me.

Q: You said that you went back to Spain. Through Tufts, or on your own?

A: During my junior year in Spain, the Dean of Undergraduate Education (Walter Swap) paid us a visit to talk about the Fulbright Program. And he gave a really convincing pitch as to the advantage of using your last couple of months in Spain to get your thoughts together in order maybe to do a senior thesis and apply for a Fulbright. And I thought wow. I knew that I wanted to go to grad school and I knew if I successfully completed a Fulbright application that it could only boost my chances to get into the grad school I wanted to get into. And doing the senior thesis was the hardest thing, but I thought I better get practice in this kind of research and writing so whether I get the Fulbright or not doing a senior thesis is probably a good idea as well. So, I made some decisions about what I would do my research on and spent my last month in Spain gathering some resources both in terms of books for my senior thesis as well as people to contact for my Fulbright application. I spent a full semester focused on getting this Fulbright application prepared. In January of 2002 there was an excursion to Havana, and my senior thesis was related to the film industry, Spanish film industry. I was able to be part of the crew that went to Havana and I did research in Cuba for my senior thesis as well.

Q: That is amazing.

A: It is amazing. Being at Tufts opened so many opportunities for me that I wouldn't have had if I had stayed at UMass or Harvard Extension, things that I would have never imagined. I always wanted to go to Cuba. I am Puerto Rican. I always wanted to compare the two islands. And so I went. I was supported by my advisor, I was supported by my professors. My advisor helped to set up appointments for me to meet people in Cuba. When I got back, I wrote my senior thesis, and the day after I presented it, I got the letter from the Fulbright commission that I got my Fulbright grant and I was able to go back to Spain.

Q: I am amazed. Because not many R.E.A.L. students opt to go abroad and become Fulbright Scholars, which is very prestigious. So, congratulations on that.

A: Thank you. There was another R.E.A.L. student who got a Fulbright and went abroad the year I did. His name is Aaron; he went to Germany. He is a little younger than I am. But it is very difficult. I know a lot of my fellow R.E.A.L. students couldn't do it because of other obligations.

Q: I would also like to ask you about your relationship with Tufts professors. How was it? Were they welcoming? Was it hard or easier to connect to them?

A: I have to say that I had nothing but positive experiences with all my Tufts professors. I think that part of it has to do with the fact that, well, Tufts has really good professors. And you know I had an interest in learning. I took an active role in classes, but I found them all very supportive. I also made it a point in the beginning of every semester to go to the office hours of my professors and let them know who I was, what I was doing, let them know that I was a R.E.A.L. student because they didn't always know. I let them know that this was meaningful to me and I think that contributed to the good relationship I had with my professors. We have different challenges as R.E.A.L. students. That does not mean they should go easier on us, they shouldn't and they don't, but it means something different for us. I think they appreciate that sacrifice.

8   Diversity, Resiliency, Legacy

Q: You graduated with honors, I think.

A: I graduated magna cum laude with thesis honors.

Q: Congratulations. What were your plans for after your Fulbright year?

A: I always had a graduate degree as a goal, even though getting my bachelor's was a very important goal for me and life changing. But I knew that I wanted a master's degree. And so in my senior year I had to decide whether I was going to be applying to grad school, or doing the Fulbright. Because I knew I could not do both, especially with also doing the regular course load.

Going to Spain on the Fulbright was an incredible year of even more opportunities opening to me. I was chosen to represent the Spanish Fulbrightees at the Western Europe Fulbright Convention. So I was able to go to Berlin as part of the experience. It was amazing. I met other Fulbrightees, some of whom I am still in touch with. And then I came back after that year and looked for work.

Q: What did you find?

A: Currently I work at Harvard University at the David Rockefeller Center for Latin American Studies and I manage events for the center. And I am taking a graduate course at the School of Education at Harvard. I plan to apply to that program and go into university administration. And my decision to go into university administration has everything to do with my experience at Tufts.

Q: How so?

A: Because, what I have been talking about all along are opportunities that were opened up for me; and that has a lot to do with the way Tufts is run. Dean Herbert is an incredible resource to the students. All the administrators there were nothing but helpful in terms of what I wanted to accomplish there. I want to be part of that, making opportunities, making sure that educational programs run well. In getting ready for this interview, I have been thinking a lot about that.

Q: Where do you see yourself in ten years?

A: I see myself as a high level administrator at a university. And I also think about part of my community, that part that looks at education in the community. I live in Cambridge. I might think about running for school committee, for example. That is in ten, fifteen years, and addressing these issues from the ground up.

Q: If you would meet a person who is thinking about going back to college or even just to start from scratch and is not sure how to do it, what would you tell that person?

A: Do it. I would absolutely encourage whoever it is. But at a time when they are ready. Because I know that I was in my 30s when I returned to school and I wasn't ready to go back before that.

Q: Is there something you would still like to add to this interview? Is there something I did not ask?

A: Just to summarize. My life really is different and better as a result of being able to go to Tufts. And not only is my life better but I do think that the people I come in contact with in my professional work and my personal life are also better off because of this. And this is for two reasons. One is my personal life. I just feel better about myself. I believe in what I can accomplish now in a way that I didn't before. And in my professional life, I have a lot more to offer because of the experiences I had at Tufts.

Benjamin Presnell

Q: Could you tell me about your job prior to deciding to go back to college?

A: Prior to entering the R.E.A.L. program, I was in the international moving and storing industry. I spoke three languages, which helped. I had been at Western Virginia University for a year and a half from 1991 to 1993. And it sort of didn't work out; I didn't know what I wanted to do in life. WVU was a party school, so you don't really pay that close attention to all of your academics. So I took a break, started working, and ended up in Boston.

And after a while, I said to myself, I have to go back, I have to complete this. It wasn't that I was unhappy. I just realized one, earning potential would be greater, and two, I felt I kind of owed it to myself to have a little bit more challenge. Sometimes you kind of feel this inferiority because you know that you are as smart as other people but because you don't have the bachelor's degree people don't treat you as if you have that sort of capability. I found that annoying, especially since a lot of people I worked with who were my superiors did not seem to understand the greater business things that were happening or international politics in general, anything that had to do with what is going on in the world. So, I started to look into programs around Boston – BU, BC, Harvard Extension, Northeastern and some others that I don't remember right now. I wanted to stay in Boston. I had just taken a job downtown, and they had a good tuition reimbursement.

12   Diversity, Resiliency, Legacy

I found the R.E.A.L. program cruising through the web, seeing what is out there. A friend of mine had come to Tufts, and he was pushing me to check it out. And the thing that appealed to me was that you are part of the regular undergraduates, unlike the other programs for adults where you are separated, where there is an odd distinction put on your academic achievement, where somehow it is not up to par as the normal university – it's Harvard Extension School, it's Metropolitan College at BU, there are these signifiers to let you know that it is just not the normal degree. Tufts does not do that, which I think is the biggest advantage of this program. You get a degree that is the same as the degree everyone else gets, and there is no special wording about it. If you try to transfer as an older student through the regular admissions process someplace, it is not the same at all. In fact, there is some sort of ageism involved in all these admission processes for transfer students because honestly you cannot just transfer in as a regular transfer student if you are over a certain age. At least not at the more selective schools.

I formed really good bonds with a lot of professors who were really interesting people, not just in class but also out of class. And they appreciated the fact that I was working part time off and on, and sometimes a lot. I was, you know, having to pay for rent in Boston. The professors appreciated the fact that the adult students take this extra effort and work so hard and so diligently to get things done and to be as good as possible. Classes were exciting, great, they were fun. I felt that I learned so much at Tufts. I think that there is such rigor here.

Q: Can you give me some examples?

A: There are just amazingly smart kids here. It was great to be in classes with these people because I noticed that the students were not really that intimidated by the fact that you are a little bit older, with a little bit different profile. And, you know, you chat with them … you don't form the same kind of friendships that of course you would have if you were their age. But everything else was pretty normal. Study groups here and there. You interact with them on campus. You fit in but at the same time you contribute to the classroom in a different way.

Q: Were you involved in extra-curricular activities?

A: I did some things with the Tufts Transgender, Lesbian, Gay and Bi-sexual Collective. Actually, last year we helped to set up a film series, an international film series, here at Fletcher. I wasn't here to do a lot of social things, which is what most of the clubs' activities are, they are social outlets for the students. I could participate in class and be in study groups, but outside of that, there was a little age gap. What I did do was to write a lot of papers. A lot of papers.

Q: What was your summer job? Was it related to what you did prior to coming to Tufts?

A: Yes, it was the job I had right before I started at Tufts. I did network administration, and financial backend products with a financial company in downtown Boston where actually some other Tufts graduates work from the year I graduated.

Q: Where are you going with your education?

A: I was lucky in that I was elected to Phi Beta Kappa. And I graduated summa cum laude, so I know that I made a good contribution to the school. And that is what plays again into being an older student. You concentrate, you can be more effective in what you do. You can manage your time better than when you were 18 years old. And I am pretty happy about the fact that I did. I was able to come out of Tufts with a high academic distinction. Which made me really happy because it made me feel that I did something really productive with the years here. And also it launched me into Fletcher, which is where I am right now. One of the best things is that once you come from Tufts it opens a lot of other doors where you can apply to places like the Sloan School at MIT and other prestigious graduate programs and they look at your age and they will be a little skeptical but then they say, oh, he went to Tufts; you have this academic credential. Which makes a huge difference when you are going forward. With the Tufts degree, when you mention it, people go, 'Oh, Tufts'; it resonates.

Q: What are your plans after graduation? You will be a double Jumbo.

A: I know a general direction. I have all these student loans which are quite massive now, so I'll talk about between now and where I would like to be in ten years. Tufts and Fletcher have given me the ability to provide a contribution to the community. I come from the industrial wasteland of northern West Virginia. It is former steel mills, pottery mills, and all sorts of places decimated by the wonderful benefits of free trade. Tufts and Fletcher gave me the analytical framework from which I can critique that and say these are the weaknesses in the system and figure ways to strengthen and create new opportunities for these communities that have been so badly affected by trade.

14   Diversity, Resiliency, Legacy

And try to go forward, strategizing our future; how do we buffer the effect of all the trade we want to partake in? I don't know if that involves politics, I don't know if that involves winning West Virginia and taking Mr. Byrd's spot. Maybe I'll develop a scholarship for a West Virginian to go to Tufts.

Q: Are you the first one in your family to get a bachelor's degree?

A: Yes. My mother attended UCLA briefly and then somewhere else. But she never finished. My dad has a high school diploma. He literally went to a one room school house in a small town somewhere until he was in 10th grade. My mom and I were a little bit more mainstream due to the fact that she actually went to a normal high school. But from my immediate family, I am the first one to have a college degree. I am actually the first one to have a master's degree in my entire family—both my mother's and father's families.

Q: Is there anything you want to add?

A: Well, if there is room for comments I would like to say that the R.E.A.L. program should be supported. Granted, you have to give them some treats in financial aid, but I still think that if you look at the other factors, there is probably a larger contribution back to the academic environment from the R.E.A.L. students, what with the relationships with the professors and the interactions with the other students. And the personal gain the R.E.A.L. students get. And if you could quantify that, I am sure that they would well exceed what you would normally expect from the regular undergraduate population.

Katerina Lucas

He came into my apartment in Munich without an invitation. Before I could comprehend what was happening, the windows were closed, my phone line was jerked out of the plug, my cell phone was in his possession, the computer almost crashed on the floor. The next thing I remember is him standing by the kitchen counter playing with a knife I had just used to slice a piece of bread before his arrival. "Nobody will care if I just kill both of us right now." Silence. "Strip!" Silence. Nothing moved. What should I do? Obey? Disobey? Run? "Do it!" I did. His following diatribe did not stay in my memory. What I do remember is the knife next to the bed. This happened seven years ago. For many years I have tried to erase it from my memory. Then, a little over a year ago, a friend told me that he holds women caught in abusive relationships in low regard. "It is their own fault," he said. I told him about my experience with an abusive boyfriend. I told him what this man had done to me after I finally had the courage to leave him and move out. My friend was fighting back tears. I am certain that he will never think the same about women like me.

I offer this experience to help educate others like my friend, and to show other women that in spite of bad experiences they can overcome fear and move on.

Interview:

Q: Katerina, can you tell me about your childhood growing up in Czechoslovakia?

16   Diversity, Resiliency, Legacy

A: I can still see how every weekend my grandfather quietly turned on the radio, pressed his ear to the speaker, and listened to the program, which always started with: "This is Radio Free Europe." Back then I did not know how much trouble my grandfather would have encountered if I had told the police officer living below us that he was listening to this radio station. Now, twenty years later, I know why the officer lived there. My family was on the list of dissenters. I, on the other hand, was a Pioneer, a ten-year-old who was proud of the friendship that Czechoslovakia had with the Soviet Union. I learned to use a rifle during P.E. classes in order to protect my country from invading capitalists. Interestingly, I didn't even know that capitalists were real people; they were the monsters under my bed. I was on my way to becoming a faithful communist.

Then, when I was twelve--November 17, 1989--the Velvet Revolution happened. My grandfather began sharing with me some events from his past. He told me about his time in the interrogation cell, about his desire to emigrate in August 1968 when the Soviet Army invaded the country, and also about the role of Radio Free Europe and its messages. This was a moment of awakening for me. Now I understood why some of his most precious books had been kept behind a curtain at home. My grandfather's Bible, Qur'an, Plato, Hume, and Orwell, along with so many other books, emerged from behind the curtain and entered into the daylight of our living room.

My life changed dramatically after 1989. I moved with my mom to Munich, Germany. During my ten-year stay in this city, I met people from all over the world. Some of them came with their families, while some of my classmates and later colleagues did not even know the whereabouts of their relatives.

Q: How did you decide to continue your education?

A: In Germany I was working for the Burger King Company, in their training department. It was a very good work environment. I had the best boss ever. She took care of all her employees beyond the usual. She sent us to seminars and cared a lot about our intellectual development. Since I was the first graduate of their training program, I was offered a job to become the trainer of the apprentices. I was the person to be called if the apprentice had trouble with school, restaurants, or even personal difficulties. I was overseeing about eighty students at that time and they were spread out all over Western Germany.

I was engaged to an American and we decided to get married. I knew that I would be moving to the U.S.. I thought that if I would ever start school again, then this would be the time to do it because I am starting fresh. But before I could start attending classes, I had to pass the GED. The toll of my transnational experiences was the fact that I had not attended my tenth and eleventh grades. After passing the GED exam, I promptly enrolled in Olympic College in Bremerton, Washington. I planned to complete my associate's degree during the summer of 2004, but this was not possible. Having an extensive experience in the nuclear field, my husband secured a position at the Nuclear Reactor Laboratory at MIT before I could achieve my goal. Since it was his dream to be at MIT, I could not say no. To be honest, it was very depressing for me to be a Navy wife. Every day I had to motivate myself to get up, make breakfast and look for a job. I applied for over a hundred jobs and received a few responses. Eventually I decided to do real estate. I took the class, passed the exam and got a job a month later. But generally, I hated my life. It was a day-to-day life without a challenge or anything to look forward to.

Q: How did you find out about Tufts?

A: I drove by one day. I saw the sign in Powderhouse Square and I remember thinking: "What is this Tufts University?" It was a completely unknown school to me. I researched it, looked at US News ranking and thought: "Hmm, I wonder if I could get in." Then I looked at the transfer student prerequisites and I didn't believe I could make it. I started browsing the web and eventually looked at transfer sites hoping to find out more and saw the R.E.A.L. program. So when I saw this I found it applied to me, so I decided to apply.

Q: Was your husband supportive about your decision to go back to school?

A: I don't think I really gave him much choice about it. He only asked how we were going to pay for it. And I said: "Well, let's see if I get admitted. Then we can talk about it." But he did help a lot. He proofread my application essays. He actually knew them by heart before I sent them away. So, he was very supportive.

Q: Were there professors that you particularly like?

A: Definitely, my two advisors. Professor Bauer in the philosophy department and Professor Lemons in comparative religion. They were both very welcoming and ready to talk to me at any time. And of course Peggy Hutaff. She is great. Generally professors here are very, very approachable. They will give you

18   Diversity, Resiliency, Legacy

feedback on your papers; they want to hear how you are doing in their class. One thing surprised me. It was okay to submit a rough draft for feedback. I had never experienced this before.

Q: Are you planning to teach philosophy?

A: Actually, my long-term goal is to teach religion in schools. I believe that an education without academic study of religions in the world is not complete. I am not talking about devotional teaching of the Bible, for example, but rather about the history, what is behind the texts, where do they come from and how they influenced humanity. Without it I don't think that we can form a complete picture about our history.

Q: Can you tell me a little about your parents?

A: My parents. Well, I don't know my father. So that is something that I won't be able to tell you about. I know his name but that is all. My mom received her master's degree in sociology in her late 30s. So she was a late starter like I am. Right now she is the executive director of a refugee camp in Czech Republic and before that she taught nursing at Charles University in Prague.

Q: Where do you see yourself if you hadn't decided to get involved in the R.E.A.L. program?

A: I probably would have left the real estate business because that was just not my calling. I would be looking for another job using my background in gastronomy and hotel management. I would probably end up there because it would be the easiest to find a job. That summer, after moving to Boston, I was offered several positions in the food industry but I wanted to break away from that. I learned what it is about, enjoyed it, then hated it, did the roller coaster ride, and wanted to learn something new. I would be bouncing from one job to another looking for a challenge.

Q: What are you doing now?

A: During my fourth semester at Tufts, after almost five years of marriage, my husband and I separated and we have since divorced. I have been accepted into the Ph.D. program at Harvard Divinity School.

Tufts and its professors intensified my interests and empowered me to major in both Comparative Religion and Philosophy. Because of my own experience, the issue of accessibility of higher education became my secondary field of interest. At the moment I am participating in a Massachusetts Campus Compact study analyzing the capacity of college access in local communities. Increasingly I became enthusiastic about the role of education, power relations in societies, and human experience under the umbrella of religion.

One day while discussing the inequalities of accessing higher education with friends, we decided to create an alumni association for the R.E.A.L. program with the purpose of allocating more funding, scholarships, and other support to the R.E.A.L. students. It is a small step towards our goal to have a larger community of older students at Tufts and thus create more diversity. I have also been working as an Area Representative for ASSE International Student Exchange Program. Every year I am responsible for foreign students coming to the U.S. living with families while attending a local high school. I find the interaction with the students and their American families to be very enriching.

Within the twenty-eight years of my life, I have lived in three countries and experienced many foreign cultures. I speak four languages and have friends from all over the Earth. I have learned to move among worlds of ethnicities, nationalities, languages, cultures and religious traditions. I feel enriched with the many differences we each bring from our backgrounds.

Nathan Alden

Q: Nathan, where did you grow up?

A: I grew up in Beverly. It's about 20 miles north of Boston. It's a good-size city, and I grew up downtown near the water. I went to public school there.

Q: Were you not a good student in high school?

A: Well, I did fairly well through the lower grades. When I went on to high school, I had a distinct problem with authority. I didn't like being told what to do. I decided that I knew what was best for me. So I sort of gave up really and just cruised through without having ambitions for college. I was really interested in my own social situation at the time and couldn't see beyond my own circle of friends. I felt like anything I needed to know, I could teach myself.

Q: What did you do after high school?

A: I met my wife while in high school. We have three children. When I graduated, she was still a senior and so I was just hanging out while she was still living at home. We decided to get a place together. Money became a factor and the word 'career' started to creep in and I had to start thinking about supporting myself. I had worked in the food service industry since I was 14 years old and had done really well. I had worked up to a management position. And then my son was born when I was 21. All of these things kept leading up to the realization that we had to start thinking about the future. I got to the

22   Diversity, Resiliency, Legacy

point where I knew that what I was doing would lead me to a point where I would hit the wall in terms of money and also personal satisfaction. I started to think about other options and just decided for the fun of it to take some classes at a community college and see what I could do. And also to prove to myself that I was capable of earning more than Cs and Ds, which is what I was getting in high school. So I took a full semester at North Shore Community College at the Beverly Campus and I earned As in all of my classes. I said: "Wow, great! I can do it." And then just sort of forgot about it for a while because when you are doing ok in terms of money – at least by my standards at the time – and then you stop it for a while and focus on school, all of a sudden you are back to really having to scrounge for money.

Good grades are their own rewards but unfortunately they don't reap immediate dividends. And so I went back to working for a while. I had reached a point where I was the general manager of a couple of locations for a restaurant chain. But finally I decided that I was not going to be able to do that forever and needed to be more challenged. I needed to really test my own limits and apply myself. So I went back to the community college and that is when I started to think about 4-year colleges.

Q: How did you find out about the R.E.A.L. program?

A: Interestingly enough, NSCC has this program called 'Motivation to Education' for people who are interested in college but don't really know where to go. That is how I found out about the R.E.A.L. program. It is pretty unique. It is not like there are a lot of schools that offer programs like this, especially schools like Tufts.

Q: How did you find the classes at Tufts compared to a community college?

A: Very different. Much harder but I expected that.

Q: So what did happen after Tufts?

A: Well, I graduated in 2004. I took it easy in the beginning of that summer and did some job searching toward the middle of the summer. By the end of the summer I started panicking. I had this idea because I made good grades here and had my priorities straight and a good head on my shoulders that people were going to be banging down my door to hire me. Fortunately, I was hired as a temp at the same place where I am still today for biotech. And that was good. I worked for a while before I got to the point where I said: "Well,

I'm never going to reach my full potential without a higher degree." So now I am in my second semester in a master's program. I did an awful lot of soul searching before deciding that I would go for the master's program versus the doctorate right now.

Q: Looking back at your time at Tufts, do you feel that coming here was the right decision? And was it worth all the difficulties that you had to overcome?

A: Absolutely. Thinking back, it really was my only option. I mean, of course there were other options but to be where I am today, it was the only real option. I am very, very glad I did it; it has done nothing but good for me. I have gotten everything that I expected out of it and more. You never know what you are going into, but I had certain core expectations and I have met all those in terms of being able to come to a top-notch school and to prove to myself and the world that I'm capable of doing this. I think that is one of the biggest selling points for this program to professors and anyone who has contact with the R.E.A.L. students. From what I have heard and seen, we are an asset because we come with a different perspective on life. We have already been out there and been through the trial by fire. So, we have some wisdom to impart. I felt very much advantaged for having had that during my studies.

Q: If you would compare the Nathan prior to Tufts to the Nathan of right now, how would those two people be different? Or the same.

A: If I were to make a contrast, I would say that I am certainly much wiser having come through the curriculum here and having had such an exposure to so many different subjects and cultures. Having come through Tufts, I am now able to see the world in a way that I never could have before. I feel that before I was almost sheltered. Coming to Tufts was my gateway to the world.

Tyler Dennison

Q: Tyler, could you please tell me what life was like for you after high school?

A: I graduated from high school in 1996 and the following spring I enlisted in the Air Force. I spent four years in the Air Force flying a cargo plane. I got out in March 2004 and moved to Boston. Originally, I was from the South Shore. When I moved to Boston, I immediately began to work in the restaurant industry. Later, I started taking classes at Bunker Hill Community College.

Q: You said that prior to going to college you were in the restaurant business. What was it like for you?

A: It was a struggle. I got a job bartending without any experience at a pretty high-end place and it was just a struggle not to get fired every day for the first six months. But it got me motivated. A lot of the people in the field, in Boston anyway, have either been to college, or are going, or are pursuing grad degrees. So it was definitely good to be around people who were more educated than myself. Especially coming from an enlisted position in the military. But at the same time, it was hard to stay out of the lifestyle and not go out too much, to remain focused on my goal. I broke my hand in September 2001 just as I started Bunker Hill and since I didn't think that work would be flexible with school, I quit. In college, I had to start with math because I was behind. In daily life, well, I would have to study a few hours in the morning, then I would have lunch and maybe exercise a little and by three o'clock I would have to be

25

26   Diversity, Resiliency, Legacy

at the bar until I got out at 1 am. And then repeat the process the next day. I didn't have much free time.

Q: What was your plan in going back to school?

A: I had pretty modest goals. I thought that being in the military was going to get me a little bit further in people's eyes than it did. So initially, I went to Bunker Hill because when I went to the open admissions interview at UMass Boston, the counselor said that due to my bad grades in high school there was no way they could let me into UMass Boston. And also that he would be surprised if I could handle the workload at Bunker Hill. That was pretty traumatizing. So I started off with small goals. I mean just dealing with the bureaucracy at Bunker Hill was a huge pain.

Q: Did you think that you could do it?

A: I wasn't sure, to be honest. I wasn't positive. I knew that I wasn't stupid but at the same time, college seemed kind of like an impossible dream. It didn't seem like something that would necessarily happen to me. When I started Bunker Hill, I was planning on doing two years there and getting the automatic acceptance to go to UMass Amherst. I thought that I could get a 3.0 or something to automatically transfer. I thought that was in my reach but that it would be a struggle. I certainly would not have believed you if you would have told me five years ago that I would end up at Tufts.

Q: How was your start at Bunker Hill?

A: Well, it was a struggle to get back into studying. I had not had to study in a long time. Basically, I had never studied in my life. It was difficult. Luckily I had to start off at a pretty low level in math at which I am not that bad. I realized I was more motivated than these kids. I started to be a little bit more confident and just felt better about the whole thing.

Q: So how did you hear about the R.E.A.L. program?

A: I had a friend at Bunker Hill who was a really smart woman. We would chat and sort of fantasize about going to a good college. She mentioned that some people could get into Tufts, that they had this special program, which she qualified for but the math is impossible and you have to take all this language and it is really hard to get into. So I never realistically thought about it. But then I saw a Tufts employee at a college fair day at Bunker Hill and I picked up an application. But I didn't seriously think about it too much. And then I had an epiphany about a week before the application was due. I decided I was going to apply instead of just going to UMass. So the first time I talked to Dean Herbert was actually asking her for an extension. I had to get my application done in about a week, which was stressful, but it turned out to be okay. I just woke up one day and decided to apply, to give it a shot.

Q: What was it like after you learned that you were in?

A: Oh, it was amazing. It was one of the best days in my life. Not many people in my family have gone to college. And growing up around Tufts, I mean anywhere Tufts is a big deal, but especially around here, Tufts has more of an international reputation. But growing up around here, people would always say: "You know, Tufts, that's where you go if you want to be a doctor." It is a big deal, you know. I went out for a celebratory dinner with my father. It was great. I was on top of the world.

Q: How was your transition to Tufts?

A: I was intimidated by the kids. I had a writing class and these kids were seven years younger than me but all so intelligent, well-spoken, well-read, bringing up philosophers that I had never heard of in casual conversations. It was intimidating and I realized pretty quickly that good writing at a community college was not good writing at Tufts. I mean I had a 4.0 at Bunker Hill and in my first writing assignment at Tufts I got a C. That was horrifying. I realized that I was going to have to work a lot harder.

Q: Did you have to work while you were at Tufts?

A: I was always a full-time student but I had a plethora of jobs over the three years I was there. I worked in retail up to about thirty hours a week. I had a fairly hard workload. But it was a nice and relaxed job so it wasn't too bad. The summers I bartended, I did real estate, I worked in a gym, a little bit of everything. Whatever I could find. Although, I wish I had pursued an internship.

Q: Other than the first semester, did you experience other challenges?

A: Yeah, definitely. It was full of challenges. On the other hand, I'm lucky in the sense that I got money from the military, which made it a lot more comfortable for me. I don't know how I would have done it otherwise. So I

28   Diversity, Resiliency, Legacy

think I had it a little easier than other people. But in terms of challenges – sure. Actually, all of the English professors at Tufts were great. I didn't have one that I wasn't really impressed by. Sometimes they are operating at a level that is so much above you so you have to play catch up all the time just to have an idea of what is going on. It was always challenging. Every new class was a challenge. And the studying involved, oh my god, I had no idea that I was capable of studying like that. Of course, now that I am in law school (at Boston University) I realize it wasn't that bad.

Q: Was law school always a goal, or something you decided you wanted to do halfway through?

A: It is something that I always hoped would be a possibility. It just grew and started to make more sense. I mean by the time I graduated, I was 27. I guess the idea of making money started to appeal to me and so first semester during my senior year I started applying to a bunch of law schools. I figured that since I was an English major that I was pretty well prepared. I could write really well.

Q: Is there anything you would like to add about your experience of the R.E.A.L. program?

A: Well, I wrote Dean Herbert an email probably about four months ago when it had really sunk in. I just couldn't speak any more highly about the program. It is such an amazing opportunity. It changed my life. I have a confidence now that was never there before. And I was so intellectually stimulated over those three years that I just think about the world in a completely different way now. I apply what I learned. I apply it to everything. Every decision I make in life, my education comes into play. And I don't think I could have gotten a better one anywhere.

Joanne Walker

I grew up in the North of England and was happy to be sent to boarding school at the age of thirteen. I had hoped to attend the year before but I failed the entrance examination. My admittance that year, as prescribed by the headmistress, was dependent on a 'serious and sustained course of tuition in mathematics' during the summer before my arrival. Alas, it didn't help much. My school reports were filled with exasperated comments like 'Joanne does not concentrate' and 'I do wish she would sit still!' This is all the more damning given the fact that my school was not, at that time, known for its academic rigor. I left school with five Ordinary levels in subjects like scripture and home economics.

Perhaps I should give myself a big pinch to make sure I'm not dreaming... No, still here.

As I write, I am in my office at Brandies University's Psychological Counseling Center. On the walls, I am proud to show off my Tufts diploma (pinch, pinch, cum laude), my degree for my doctorate in psychology (my thesis was a secondary data analysis) and my certificate from Massachusetts General Hospital/Harvard Medical School attesting to my successful completion of a three-year post-doctoral clinical fellowship.

For me, university had been out of the question as I lacked the necessary examinations. I felt a mixture of envy and shame as my friends went off to study interesting things in new places and my destination was secretarial school. Eventually, I found my sea legs and started working for a London art dealer. This began a life-long passion for English watercolors and Old Master Drawings which in turn led me to spend the following decade living and working in Florence and Paris. I was delighted to find that I had a natural aptitude for wheeling and dealing in the art market, albeit at a modest level.

I soaked up the culture, language and mores until my Italian friends would tease that I was more Italian than they were. Eventually this language ability was strong enough to permit me to enroll in several classes at the University of Florence and later at the Sorbonne.

Somehow, whilst sitting in those vast amphitheatres with the hundreds of other students, I realized how little I knew about anything and I longed to gain a little more understanding of the world I lived in. Simply put, I realized that there was no discipline to my thinking and no coherence to my learning. And then there was another thing. I had the vague and quaint notion that I wanted to 'help people,' an idea that had been fuelled from many years of voluntary work.

It quickly became apparent that America truly was a land of opportunity and that there were several universities who would consider my previous training and course work rather than traditional expectations. The R.E.A.L. program stood out amongst all of the other programs, as it was the only institution that would allow me to be an equal member of the community. I would have the same opportunities and challenges as my younger classmates: we would take the same courses and work towards the same degree. I was eager to be part of an academic community that believed in a truly diverse student body without prejudice against age. It was clear that Tufts would bestow neither privilege nor penalty for being a good 15 years older than the average freshman. I was also attracted to the community of R.E.A.L. students. It was evident that they cared for each other and that there was a wealth of shared knowledge on how to thrive in this exhilarating and challenging environment. I quickly learned to get over being mistaken for a professor. Oh the looks I would get when entering the first class of the semester and taking a seat amongst the rank and file!

Curiously, the most precious and influential friendships I formed at Tufts were with the 'regular' students. I had much to learn from them. They were immensely disciplined and experienced study machines and they taught me with great good humor how to make it academically. And they seemed to enjoy having a classmate who they felt was young enough to remember and relate to the acute pains and pleasures of early adulthood without being 'so old' that I couldn't possibly understand. Fond memories return of long hours in the bowels of Tisch where the conversations would shift seamlessly between coursework, social pressures and heartbreak. No small coincidence, perhaps, that today the highlight of my professional week is providing therapeutic services to university students.

I am inordinately proud of my alma mater. Frequently, my association will arise in conversation with friends, colleagues or strangers recognizing the logo on my thread worn sports clothes. Identifying me as one of their cohorts by virtue of age, they may stop and ask which class I was in. Invariably they are surprised and then curious to learn that although I am in my mid 40's, I was in the class of 1998. No, I joke, I am not a twenty-something year old who has aged appallingly; I was part of the R.E.A.L. community of older students. I believe that Tufts' sponsorship of the R.E.A.L. program proves its genuine commitment to diversity in the student body whilst simultaneously promoting good will in the community.

Tufts for me was the bridge between some vague desire to work in the social services and a passionate and challenging career in psychology. Yet it has given me so much more than that. In graduate school I was lucky enough to meet my husband and last year we celebrated the birth of our daughter. I am confident that without Tufts, I would still have found a way to carve out a life of meaning but I feel that it would have been a grayer and less informed life. Thank you for this invaluable and irreplaceable opportunity.

Bernard Zirnheld

Q: Bernard, please describe a typical day for you before you decided to go back to school.

A: Oh, I took many years off. I went back to school when I was like 30 or 31. I took a good ten years off, and in that time I did a lot of community work. I was busy all the time. I was doing a lot of social justice work in Western Massachusetts. Later, I moved to Boston. I was working in public housing as a consultant. But to be honest, I didn't feel like I was doing what I really wanted to do. I felt that I would always be on the bottom tier of whatever organization I was part of. I guess going back to school was to radically reshape my life and figure out what I wanted to do.

I did two years in comparative literature immediately after high school and then dropped out. I guess I was not ready for it. I had some growing up to do first. Later, in 1997, I attended an architecture school. You could say that I was testing the waters. After that I entered the R.E.A.L. program.

Q: How did you learn about the R.E.A.L. program?

A: At first, I had no idea about the R.E.A.L. program. During the time in the architecture school, I was about ten years older than the other students. When I decided to go back, to finish my bachelor's degree, I thought that the experience would be kind of alienating. Being much older, I didn't feel like I would fit in. So, I called around to find if there were specific programs for returning adult students. I just really had a list of schools in the area and called them asking what kind of support they have for older students.

34   Diversity, Resiliency, Legacy

Q: What was attractive about Tufts?

A: I think the high standards. That was the deciding factor. I'm at Yale doing my doctorate now. Tufts was a kind of entry to an academic track at a high quality level that had a lot to do with things like my going to Yale. It was just perfect for me.

Q: You said earlier that you majored in architecture and French. How was your experience in these studies?

A: In the architecture studies, one of the professors became very much a mentor to me. The professors were really wonderful and great. They were able to talk about career choices and larger issues. My mentor was really amazing. Actually, it was not only the architecture department. The R.E.A.L. program was also an amazing support. It was really helpful to go through the entire experience with others who were also older. Especially if compared with the architecture school, where a lot of people didn't really know what to do with me. Having the first semester seminar was great; I got to know other people who returned to school and people with different life trajectories. I felt that I had a place. I felt less of a freak, I guess. And the R.E.A.L. students were so interested in what they were doing. But I think that as an older student you just are. You are focused in a different way, which also makes it enjoyable.

Q: What did you do after graduation?

A: I was working throughout my time at Tufts. After my second year, I went to Paris on the Tufts Study Abroad Program. That was an amazing experience. It was life changing. After my return and my last year at Tufts, through a contact from the architecture department, I started to work with a preservation firm. And I kept doing this for two years after graduation. I was a researcher for architectural preservation. I think the firm even worked on the Goddard Chapel at Tufts.

Q: How did you progress from this job to your graduate studies at Yale University?

A: Actually, on paper, Yale was the last place I should have come for the things I wanted to do. But the R.E.A.L. program ended up having a large influence on my deciding process because I ended up choosing a school for its environment. I really expected to go to Columbia because of the program and the place itself, but I just felt so alienated from the institution when I visited.

And the thing that really struck me at Yale was the people. It is one thing if you go to grad school when you are 22, when you can just put your whole life into it. But I was 34 when I came to grad school. I was in a relationship and also in need of maintaining certain things. I think that as an older student, I needed to be respected as a person. And Yale made that impression on me.

Q: What are your plans after your graduate program?

A: I would love to teach. But academia is so competitive since the jobs are so rare. So, I am not sure. Again, if I was 24 and could go night and day, then maybe. But I don't want it to be as time consuming as grad school. I think that I am maybe leaving the idea to work at a top tier school and think of myself as an educator at lower tiered schools. I just don't want to kill myself. My plan B is to become a librarian, live in a place I want to live in compared with having a job and living in a place where I don't want to live.

Q: Would you do it all over again?

A: I am pretty happy about the trajectory of my life. It is who I am. I just cannot imagine it any other way. It was an incredibly rich experience, being an older student.

Q: What do you think the R.E.A.L. students bring to the Tufts campus?

A: I think that we bring a more serious engagement. We are a different generation with a different set of concerns. I should also tell you that I was diagnosed HIV positive when I was 21. At the time there was no treatment. Then, later, it became available. For me the R.E.A.L. program was at the moment of my life when I thought I would not be here at the age of 30. And I made it. So, it gave me the courage to return to the world in a way and prepare for the future that I thought I would never have. The R.E.A.L. program offered a really useful transition in that sense. It really made an enormous difference in my life, and I don't think I would be on the track that I am on today without it. And the support, both financially and socially for the returning students to be among other adult students, really allowed me to stay with it and enjoy it. I am really grateful. It really changed my life.

(NOTE: Bernie was elected to the Phi Beta Kappa Society and was given the French Department award.)

Ruth

Q: Could you please describe for me a day in your life prior to starting at Tufts?

A: I was living in a three-room flat in Jamaica Plain. Then I moved to an apartment that an old drama coach of mine owned in Cambridge. You could say that I lived hand to mouth, but it certainly did not feel like that. I ate simply, I lived simply. I didn't do a lot of entertainment. I really felt that my life did not have direction but needed one. So, I had a very modest, relatively low-income life before coming to Tufts.

Q: How did you find out about Tufts?

A: I don't remember the specifics actually. I do remember vaguely about researching the school I wanted to go to and finding out about the R.E.A.L. program through that. I have the impression that I talked to Dean Connor at that point. And that she believed in me more than I believed in myself. I also talked to people at work and they encouraged me.

Q: If I can ask you, why didn't you consider going to college right after high school?

A: I did. I graduated in '74 and this was, to my recollection, early on in the days of affirmative action. I was recruited by MIT; I even received a letter from Tufts. I was recruited by Georgetown and a bunch of other schools. I had a full ride to MIT, actually. But I did not believe that I could make it at one

37

38   Diversity, Resiliency, Legacy

of those schools. My guidance counselor had said to me: "Oh, they are just using you for affirmative action. You will never make it in these schools. You will never make it through the four years of these schools. They are going to make their money on you in the first year and they will let you go. They will wash you out." And I believed him.

He said that women in my community--a small rural community in Maryland, primarily black--that for generations the women there have provided child care, done laundry. They were farmers with their husbands. They had fruit stands. And they took in ironing. And he told me that I should do laundry like all the other women in my community had done. And that was a really harsh statement as far as I was concerned. I knew that I was capable of doing more than that. I had read the encyclopedia for fun as a kid. My dad had a set of 1914 Funk and Wagnalls lying around and a more contemporary set of Scientific American. I was reading and observing, and taking in information and thinking things through. So, I did not really think that I was cut out to be a laundress.

But neither of my parents had a college education. They really didn't know what we needed to do. And my dad was unreliable and disorganized. So, even though I had scholarship offers and was being recruited by good schools, if he didn't turn in his taxes the year I needed it I lost out. They were just really confused about the process and they could not offer me much help. And I told you my guidance counselor thought I should be a laundress. So, I really was not getting much support about how to approach this process, how to get into college. And I was hindered by my father's limitations. So, I didn't go to school right away.

I ended up going to the easiest school I thought I could get into to get ready for college. I went to a community college and I was bored to tears. I really liked the reading material but was not motivated to do the work. Then I was admitted to the University of Maryland, but I left after the first semester to spend 8 months in Germany with my brother. Because he was in the military and I had the chance to go somewhere. By this time I was 19 or 20 years old, and I thought that nobody starts college at 20. And it just seemed that I would have to find some other way to make a living. So, that is a really roundabout answer. I am getting into more history than I thought I would. But, the bottom line is that I did have opportunities to go to college, but my resources, my personal resources, my family, my guidance counselor just didn't know how to get me there.

Q: But you made it to Tufts …

A: I came to Boston because I had a boyfriend here and it would get me away from home. And I had a chance to go to school. I looked into Boston University. They said that I was an underachiever. I would like to go back to BU and show them my Ph.D. ring now.

Q: Let's get back to Tufts. The first time you had to leave because your husband was accepted to grad school.

A: Yeah. I had a semester here at Tufts. I was married in November of '82. My husband had been accepted to the University of Chicago. And as a newly married couple we were trying to figure out what is the best option for us to have an enjoyable life and still accomplish our goals. I was enjoying myself but it made sense to me that I could continue doing secretarial work while he was in graduate school. That he could get through and then I could go to school after that. So, that is what we did. He got his master's in divinity and then got a fellowship to do an extra year for a master's in public policy. And that way his career interests were set so he could come back and work as a policy analyst for the Commonwealth. And I could go back to school.

Q: What did you major in at Tufts and what was your experience here?

A: I majored in Clinical Psychology. Tufts made it possible to come back. The same support I had four years earlier was still there in the form of Dean Connor and Dean Knable. And I am eternally grateful to them and to Dean Herbert. I think it was Dean Knable who told me that they needed resident directors and it would be unusual for a R.E.A.L. student to do it, but it would be possible. But actually my husband is the one who would apply for it and we were RDs the first year we were here, in Houston Hall. And that helped me to finance my education along with grants and loans.

Q: What were your plans for after graduation?

A: I knew that I wanted to go to graduate school. You don't get a psychology undergraduate degree and expect to get a job. In my mind, having been in the working world and having talked to other people with a psychology degree, I knew if I wanted to accomplish my own goals, I would need a graduate degree. And not just a master's degree, but I would need a Ph.D.

Q: And you accomplished your dream.

40   Diversity, Resiliency, Legacy

A: Yes. I went to the University of Michigan. I received my Ph.D. in 2002. I work as a staff psychologist in the California Medical Facility in Vacaville, California, which is a prison hospital, so I am working with psychiatrically impaired and incarcerated men. And specifically I am in the administrative segregation unit, which is more commonly termed 'the hole' by people who know prison. So, these are offenders who have broken more rules while they were in prison. They are child molesters, or they have killed a child … and those men are particularly vulnerable to be injured and killed by other inmates if that becomes public information.

I became a psychologist so I can work with people who need help. And these men definitely need help. Between my training at Tufts and my training at Michigan, I think of the psychologies holistically--the different levels of brain functions--I think about special contexts that help to form people and genetic contributions, about all the different contributions that come together, behavioral decisions that made them the way they are, to discover how they decided to become violent rather than resilient.

Q: What are your plans for the future? Would you like to stay in this job?

A: I have to commute an hour and a half each way to get there. And I am a little old for sitting in my car that long. … So, I am going to work closer to home. Now that I am licensed, I am going to start a very part-time private practice. Also, I really want to teach and I need to write. I need to do research.

Q: I have one last question. Do you enjoy your life better than before? Is there a qualitative difference?

A: I do. I do enjoy my life better because I feel like I am fulfilling my purpose. I always wanted to help people but I thought that I cannot really help people until I am solid myself. And I feel like now I am in a stronger position to help people the way I want to.

Delis Etienne

I was born in the back country of Haiti in 1977, where I now realize education was very rudimentary. My studies were interrupted after my third grade when I became very ill. In December 1988, I became completely blind. To make a long story short, a year later I came to the United States, where I discovered that my blindness had been caused by a brain tumor. I underwent a successful operation, but due to my condition, I could not return to Haiti.

In 1990, I began my education at Perkins School for the Blind, a big challenge because I could only speak Creole. Nine years later, I graduated with a high school diploma, and was advised to continue my studies at a community college. I enrolled at the North Shore Community College, where I had a wonderful experience. During the course of my last year, my teachers suggested that I should apply to Tufts University as a R.E.A.L. student. I followed their advice, and visited Tufts, where I felt most welcome. During my visit, I spoke with some students; they all had excellent comments about the university. The best comment I heard from the students was: "The teachers are very caring."

Because of my blindness, I had to be realistic in choosing my curriculum. Tufts University has a program, international relations, that offered me the chance to pursue my interests fully. I worked hard and got good grades. The support services I received at Tufts helped me to succeed. I never want to forget where I came from and so now I work with Dr. Paul Farmer's organization in Cambridge, Partners in Health. I am able to fulfill my goal of helping people in Haiti.

Kathryn Sutton

Graduating from Tufts University at 53 years old filled my soul in a way that nothing else could. My brothers had all attended college and I felt left behind because I had married young and college was not an option at the time. In 1974 my then husband and I bought a VW van and spent a year driving from Cairo to Capetown. The defining event in my life was time that we spent with the Samburu tribe in northern Kenya. They were very poor yet so kind and generous, sharing their food and their time with us.

I started asking the question "Why aren't I reading in the New York Times what we as Americans can learn from Africans rather than the other way around?" I returned to the US, had two boys, divorced my husband and raised my children alone. I was a small business consultant who helped people start or strengthen existing businesses. I had always told my sons that after they graduated college I was planning on going back to Africa to help women entrepreneurs. My youngest joined the US Marines in 1999 and I sent out my resume to a number of different organizations with ties in Africa, but not one of them would interview me because I didn't have a college degree.

A client of mine strongly suggested that I go to the local community college and take a college class. I was terrified, as I didn't think that I could write and couldn't imagine being a student again after so many years. But I did sign up for a history course and fell in love with learning. After a number of twists and turns I sent an email to the heads of IR at Georgetown, Yale, Harvard and Tufts and it was John Jenke at Tufts who responded the next day, telling me that I was a good candidate for the R.E.A.L. program.

Attending Tufts for three years was much more than just an academic experience – it was a lesson in living that will help me always. I made many friends among the younger students and always enjoyed their enthusiasm

44   Diversity, Resiliency, Legacy

when they would help me study. Many of the professors have become close friends of mine – they listened to my hopes and dreams and my confusion as to how to move forward. They helped me to get the utmost out of my time at Tufts. I learned how to take notes, how to ask questions, how to approach others who had knowledge that I wanted. I loved the small classes and the caring of the entire staff at Tufts. I always felt, and still do, that everyone was very much a team. But most of all I gained self respect and dignity – I don't ever have to apologize again for not having a college degree. I am proud of the hard work that I put in to attain that degree. There were times that I was ready to give up, but the students and professors helped me through those hard times.

In my senior year, I applied for a Fulbright. I wasn't chosen, but my youngest son said, "Mom, obviously you're meant to do something else – you just don't know what yet." I had planned to do my Fulbright in Tanzania, so I went to Zanzibar to spend a month studying Kiswahili. I am still here over three years later and I plan on making Zanzibar my permanent home. I have found my place in the world for now and I have a purpose here.

I became involved with ZAPHA+ (Zanzibar Association of People Living with HIV/AIDS) and have been instrumental in getting anti-retroviral medications to Zanzibar through the Clinton Foundation HIV/AIDS Initiative. I was the "People Living with HIV/AIDS" advisor to the Clinton Foundation for two years. I am still and will always be a consultant to ZAPHA+ . They have gone from 35 members in January 2005 to almost 500 now. They are great advocates for people living with HIV/AIDS in all of Zanzibar and beyond.

My next step is to start my own foundation in the US. It will be called Participate Now! We will empower people to become participants rather than just recipients. We will live among the people and listen to them to find out what their needs are and how those needs can best be met. We will work on very small scale projects that can be successful and sustainable. I would not have been able to accomplish half of this if I hadn't been a student in the R.E.A.L. program at Tufts. As we say in Kiswahili – nashukuru sana – I am very grateful. I urge anyone who has a dream of attending college late in life to pursue that dream – don't ever give up because you never know what you may learn.

Jane Wahome

Tufts stimulated my senses with the excitement of all future professional life had to offer. I was given the opportunity to engage in hands-on biotech research in the Chemical and Biological Engineering Department. A writing class uncovered within me a love for composing poems. By inviting speakers such as Desmond Tutu to address students, the university instilled in me the need to respond to the political tension and turmoil in the world with an open mind and a spirit of understanding and dialogue. Through speaking with Nutrition Center graduate students who had worked on the field in famine-stricken and war-torn regions of the world, I was exposed to the extreme needs of humanity. These discussions aided in cementing within me the desire to serve both my local and global community in whatever small or large way I may find myself able.

The professors and administrators I interacted closely with were the most intelligent, interesting yet kind and humble individuals I have ever come across. They were excellent role models for me and I am still struggling to live up to their example. At Tufts, I accomplished my life-long dream of becoming a chemical engineer. This education has enabled me to follow my heart's desire to spread the word of renewable energy and to make a meaningful contribution to the biopharmaceutical industry. In addition, it has provided me with financial freedom, the opportunity of lifelong learning and the luxury to dream.

While at Tufts, I co-founded the Swahili Club. It was a place where students could learn about the different countries in which Kiswahili is spoken. They could learn the basics of the language from students who came from or had visited these countries. Many members had spent a summer or semester in Kenya or Tanzania and wished to maintain the Swahili they had acquired

46   Diversity, Resiliency, Legacy

there. Some were taking a Tufts Swahili course and wanted to converse. Other students visited the club in preparation for trips to Africa. At the meetings, we ate food from Eastern Africa and listened to African music; we shared our experiences from that part of the world and spoke some Swahili.

But most of all when I think of Tufts, my heart is warmed by the secure and cozy family atmosphere of caring and friendship that I experienced there, that and the beauty of the Hill in Fall.

The R.E.A.L. program provided much of the cozy family atmosphere. The participants of this small group were very interesting and diverse in their views and life experiences but they were uniform in their brilliance. I was very honored to be considered part of this gathering. During the weekly meetings in our first semester and at other points during my time at Tufts, I was glad to share my views and background, as, among other things, an African female and aspiring engineer. I hope this impacted them in some positive way.

Ofir Braverman

Six years ago, I was sitting in my office contemplating whether or not to make a major change in my life. I was 27 years old, working for a software company in Israel, living a good life and enjoying a good salary. However, something was missing. Throughout my twenties I had always wanted to get a bachelor's degree in philosophy. It was one of my passions and a dream that I always kept postponing.

I used to spend my weekends browsing through websites of various universities in the US. Tufts was always on my list since it was ranked as one of the best schools in the nation and had an unbelievable philosophy department. However, being in my late 20's I felt reluctant to make a move; studying with younger students did not seem the right thing to do at my age. It is only after learning about the R.E.A.L. program that I actually worked up the courage to apply.

For me, a college degree is much more than just another one of those 'adult education' programs. Going to school means spending time in the classroom and being around other individuals who are going through the same learning experience in order to achieve their educational goals. The R.E.A.L. program was the perfect choice – it was the best of both worlds.

Luckily I was accepted and decided to give notice at my job. It wasn't an easy thing to do, venturing into the unknown; a new country, new surroundings, a new way of life – but I decided to go and give it my best shot. Looking back, it is funny how much thought went into making that decision – especially now, after the fact, when I realize that this was one of the best decisions that I have ever made in my life.

The R.E.A.L. program helped me get through college, meet people who were also passionate about getting their bachelor's degree, and make new friends.

48   Diversity, Resiliency, Legacy

It also enabled me to explore other academic avenues and get a well-rounded education. Going through school, I realized that being an older student was a great advantage; students in the R.E.A.L. program were passionate about their studies and really wanted to make a change in their lives.

My experience at Tufts has totally reshaped my life; my career is on a new exciting path and I am no longer another person without a college degree. But most important of all, the R.E.A.L. program has helped me take advantage of all that Tufts had to offer and to achieve my academic goals at my own pace. Had I not applied to the R.E.A.L. program I would still be sitting on the same old office chair, contemplating change.

Hiro Nakajima

Graduating from college was one of my biggest goals and the R.E.A.L. program at Tufts University gave me that chance. To achieve my goal, I made it through full of pride. I love to face new challenges such as creating new businesses, relocating to unknown places in foreign countries, getting a helicopter license and so on. The more I accomplish my goals, the more confidence I gain. Once people called me a successful businessman. However, I felt that something was missing: knowledge in general and education. Since I was a kid, I hated reading and writing even in my own language, Japanese. Until the age of 34, I had stayed away from my weakest point because I believed that education was not necessary in my life. However, the older I got and the more people I met, the more I felt I was ashamed of myself. I did not know what was going on in the world. I knew nothing at all. Moreover, I had lived in the United States for several years at that time and I could not even speak and understand English properly.

Although I had attended a couple of other schools, Tufts University was the best choice for me. Even though classes at Tufts were harder and I tore my hair out sometimes, I learned and gained quite a lot from them. Because of my English barrier, I spent more time studying than anybody else; my old and stubborn brain did not want to accept new information.

However, I am now glad and proud of myself. Even though I had a hard time on campus, I benefited more ways than I expected. I am now able to read, write and speak English. I can express myself so that I feel I have more freedom and confidence. Because of learning history and culture from

50   Diversity, Resiliency, Legacy

school, I was able to adapt to the new society. Now, I am very comfortable living in my new paradise, Maui in Hawaii. I have now better economical eyes: my assets continue to grow by themselves. And finally, my dream came true. I wrote two books and they became bestsellers in Japan. The R.E.A.L. program at Tufts University completely changed my entire life. I thank Tufts University and Dean Jean Herbert. With pride, I will continue to pursue my next challenges.

Eri Takashima

I can still clearly remember the day when I first learned about the R.E.A.L. program. I was perusing college options books at the Harvard Coop. Among them was 'The Adult Students' Guide, 2nd Edition', by Leigh Grossman and Lesley McBain. The R.E.A.L program was exactly what I was searching for; it enrolled adult students in Tuft's undergraduate program and this meant that I could participate in regular undergrad student organizations including the orchestra and would have access to all university facilities. I could study at Tufts University as an official undergraduate, even at this late stage in my college career if accepted! When I graduated from Cambridge Rindge & Latin High School in 1998, I went on to study biochemistry at Suffolk University. It was with no hesitation that I chose biochemistry as my major as I had a dream of getting into vet school and helping animals one day. Also, my father is a biomedical engineer so I have to admit, I wanted to follow in his footsteps too. However, I always had a passion for art and music but I believed that I should major in something practical.

At Suffolk, I soon discovered that I had no interest in biology and chemistry…I was bored. Add to this, because Suffolk was a commuter school, it lacked a sense of community and there was not much campus life. I lost my focus in school not only because of my lack of interest in the sciences but because I had to return to Japan several times to care for my ailing grandfather. As a result, I took a leave from college in 2001 and later I continued my education at Harvard Extension School and Harvard Summer School, which I thoroughly enjoyed.

Attending Harvard Extension School was interesting and quite satisfying but since the classes were offered in the evenings and the students were mostly working adults, I felt I was missing a complete college experience.

Also, Harvard Extension School underscored its boundary between "real" Harvard students, faculty and official activities and those for extension or night school students. I had always yearned to join a school orchestra because I had played violin in orchestras from middle school straight up to my senior year in high school and this meant a lot to me. I knew if I was accepted into the R.E.A.L. program I would be able to audition for the Tufts Symphony Orchestra (TSO). I also craved a college experience on a large 'leafy' campus with international students and plenty of student activities and seminars.

I was delighted when I received my acceptance letter to Tufts R.E.A.L. program. When I started at the program in January 2003, I encountered Malka Yaacobi, the TSO Director, and her husband, Arie Yaacobi, who became my violin teacher throughout my two years at Tufts. I am still in contact with this wonderful couple

The students in the R.E.A.L. program were also helpful in that they shared their experiences with me and helped me navigate the system. I was able to graduate in two years with a B.A. in Child Development. During this time, I encountered many wonderful professors in the Child Development, Art, and Music departments. Also, I made several good friends with teachers and peers, something I will treasure for the rest of my life.

It's been two years since I graduated. I returned to Japan to help care for my family. During this time, I took up mountain climbing! Now that I've returned to the U.S., I am ready to take the next step. Tufts has given me a solid base of education, which will enable me to pursue a master's degree, and my interests in the arts. My experience at Tufts has also given me confidence in the academic realm which I was miserably lacking before I attended. I am grateful to the R.E.A.L. program for providing me with such a rich experience, which I attribute mainly to the fact that there is no boundary between regular undergraduate students and older returning students. It gave me exactly what I desired, a "R.E.A.L." college experience.

Tobias Bonthrone

Q: Why did you start your education later in your life?

A: I found myself in November 2005 moving to Medford, and I knew that Tufts was a very reputable college. I began to explore options to return to college. I had never planned to take as long a break as I did. I quit after two years at King's College in London. I was taking a degree in war studies. And it was meant to be a bridge to either returning to King's College with more vigor, or starting a new degree course elsewhere in Britain. After being out of college for two years, I found out that I just could not wait. So I started to look at colleges nearby.

Tufts, due to the proximity and its reputation, was my first choice. One big problem for me was funding because I am married and I don't have any parental backing, so the first thing I did before even considering applying to Tufts was to call the financial aid office. And I explained my situation to them that I am a little bit older, and I am married, I am 23. They told me about the R.E.A.L. program and it really seemed to meet my needs. What the R.E.A.L. program offered to me was a chance to actually make something of those previous two years in college. In addition to being at Tufts University. I finally knew what I wanted in life. I knew I needed that degree. And I couldn't wait to return to a learning environment. All these things came together and that is why the R.E.A.L. program to me was ideal.

Q: Why did you leave King's College?

54   Diversity, Resiliency, Legacy

A: I found that degree didn't really suit the intellectual path that I was following. It suited my professional path. I had spent the two years previous in Britain doing A-levels. In hindsight, what I needed more was something like the American system, which obviously does not exist in Britain. I was in a course where you had only about 8 hours of teaching a week, and that left me with too much free time. I needed a structured environment. I joined the military reserve, the army reserves in Britain, and became fit. In terms of academic interest, I found my focus going towards psychology. I became very interested in psychology through the military; why do people do this and that. My course in war studies did not account for how people really think. And that was the main cause of my discontent with King's.

I got the chance of doing military service full time as an officer. I was doing promotion courses with the reserve officer training corp. It was a risky proposal because when I started this process, I was a geek, I was almost the antithesis of a military officer, and I had these two years to transform myself into somebody else. And I did find out that I could become a military officer and I was given two choices: I could go the regular route, but I also qualified for a brand new program which allowed me to take a gap year in college. That was really hard to get because there were only four spaces available. But I weighed those two options and decided to go for the gap year because it would allow me to return to college, it would allow me the flexibility of doing that gap year, get the experience, and I would have no commitment afterwards even though I would probably continue my career in the military.

Q: What did you do in that time?

A: I spent a month at Sandhurst, which is like West Point, doing a quick commission course. After a month at Sandhurst, I found myself traveling to Cypress with a Scottish infantry unit called the Royal Highland Fusiliers. I spent about a month in training and one day out of the blue I get a phone call, and like this I am transferred to a new unit in a different company. And I am told, yeah, you are it. You are the new platoon commander for six platoons. And good luck. Exercise starts tonight. I expected to do another training course before I got a chance to do this, which would have given me more infantry specific command skills. Usually you are given a command after 12 months at Sandhurst and another six months of training in a specific job.

This was in November 2003. A few weeks later we found out that my platoon was deploying to Iraq, which caused difficulties for me because my contract did not allow me to go. Nonetheless, it fell on me to co-organize the training for my soldiers who would deploy in March 2004, but I would have to make sure that they were properly trained for this deployment. And that is what I did. I had to co-organize with the other two platoon commanders, write the schedules for training and what skills they would need. Eventually we did it. We did pretty well on the final competition where every platoon competed against the others in various skills like running, and marching, and shooting and we won everything. It was now about late February. I was a platoon commander for about four months. At the same time, I was the company's educational officer.

Q: What does this mean?

A: This meant that I had to advise them all on how to take advantage of the GI bill. Except that in the U.S. the GI bill was $40,000 and for them it was about $4000. One of my primary achievements was getting one of my soldiers to apply to a psychology degree program via the Open University, which is Britain's premier distance learning program. And others were going to do their A-levels, their high school diploma, GED that kind of thing. So, I had mainly these two focuses. I had the fighting and I had the education.

This is in March 2004. There were four platoons in my company; three were going to Iraq, one was going to the Falkland Islands. The Falkland Islands did not sound that great to me because it is kind of the armpit of the world. Except for the penguins and land mines. I decided that I wanted something different. I responded to an article in Soldier's Magazine, which is the British army propaganda magazine. It is like army <u>Pravda</u>. One of the articles was by a retired colonel looking for an adventurer to explore a 5000-foot gorge in the middle of South America. I became entranced by this idea. I flew to Britain on my way to the Falkland Islands, to interview with this retired colonel, who was very much a remnant of British colonialism. The kind of man who wears khaki trousers, khaki shirt and khaki pith helmet.

He offered me the job and I willingly accepted. I had a month before the expedition started, so I had to fly to the Falklands. I didn't really have anything to do there because I would not be there long enough. I did not have any duties. I trained arriving air force crews on basic infantry tactics. The rest of the time I locked myself in my room and I wrote my very first screenplay. I don't really know where this desire came from. I think it had to do a lot with my first two years in college. And I just started to write night and day in the Falklands, just like that.

Q: What was it about?

56   Diversity, Resiliency, Legacy

A: It was about a bunch of students, each based on a different friend of mine. And it was rubbish. Then it was time to leave the Falklands and fly to Bolivia. I spent about 7 out of the 12 weeks just traveling throughout the country. There were two parts of this expedition. One group was going down the Rio Grande in rafts and one was re-supplying this group and providing aid to the villages and that kind of stuff, looking for Indiana Jones type temples and lost treasures. I was part of that group.

I was doing a lot of soul searching because I didn't know what else to do with my life. The other people were berating me for lack of imagination and really pushing me to apply to a university. We found an Internet café with international phone lines. I ended up applying to Royal Holloway College in London, which is my dad's alma mater. I applied to psychology and was accepted, all from Bolivia. Two days after I was accepted, I met my future wife. She is an American who was in Rio Grande just for a few days. She was a Peace Corps trainee. I knew in an instant that I had met someone special. Only two weeks after we met, we became engaged. I was expected to go to Holloway and wait for my fiancé who was going to be in Bolivia for the next two years. But we said, Let's just do something together, and so, we ended up both leaving Bolivia.

We ended up moving to the States because she could not find a job in Britain and that is why I had to give up my place at the university in London. We have been in the Boston area since 2005. As soon as I got my green card, we moved here, and I started looking at Tufts.

Q: But it did work out.

A: It did. In fact, during my time in Cypress, I would sometimes fly to Germany and visit the German Leadership College; I would fly to Sweden and meet with a group of people there who were part of the Swedish National Defense College. I did this as part of a research group who specialize in leadership development with people like myself, young officers. I have continued working with this group and we have recently finished our research. We are going to publish our results soon. It's one of the reasons I came to Tufts. Tufts has Dean Sternberg, who is the Dean of the School of Arts and Sciences. He is bringing the Pace Center from Yale, which has a leadership study among other things. They have done things with the military, and this would be the perfect, perfect avenue for me to continue the kind of stuff I'm interested in. So, … once again this is just another proof that Tufts is a wonderful university with lots of ambition in the right circumstances for people like myself. I think that the R.E.A.L. program is an obvious tribute to that.

Scott Arsenault

Q: Scott, could you please describe a day in your life prior to college? What kind of job did you have?

A: Prior to college, I was in the US Marine Corps, an electrician, and a native of Somerville.

Q: What made you decide to go back to college?

A: I worked in construction, but knew I wanted to be on the white-collar end of construction. So I decided to get a degree in Electrical Engineering and to be poor for a few years while being a full time student.

Q: Was your family supportive?

A: Yes, but being the first in the family to get a degree, I'm not sure they fully understood until I graduated and landed a great career with the US Coast Guard.

Q: How did you hear about the Tufts R.E.A.L. program and why did you decide to apply?

A: I was a full time student at UMass Boston. A classmate of mine at UMass learned of the program, applied and was accepted into the R.E.A.L. program.

58   Diversity, Resiliency, Legacy

She encouraged me to do the same. Her name is Christine Mello, who also graduated from Tufts as a R.E.A.L. student.

Q: Was your decision to come to Tufts a difficult one?

A: It was difficult only in the perspective of finances. It was very expensive vs. going to a state school. But I made it work. My first semester was especially busy and difficult. Engineering is a tough major.

Q: Were you involved in any research? Clubs? Other campus activities.

A: Holding a job and going to school didn't allow for much time to do anything else, so no.

Q: What were your plans, your thoughts during your last semester at Tufts? About a job? Grad school?

A: The plan was to have an easy last semester (which I did) to allow me to focus on getting job applications out. One of the reasons engineering was attractive to me was the fact that I could make more money with a B.S.E.E. than a liberal arts major with a master's (or even a Ph.D.). That proved to be true. I never had any ambition towards grad school. I had a hard enough time getting through my B.S. degree. I still have no regrets and think I made the right choice.

Q: Did you have any difficulties at Tufts?

A: Yes, the age gap. I didn't feel as though I fit in with my peers (non R.E.A.L. peers). I did make friends, but the age gap made it awkward at times. I was a Marine Corps veteran going to a top-notch university with a bunch of kids, very smart kids.

Q: How did the Tufts R.E.A.L. program change your family's life?

A: It allowed me to get a great education from a prestigious school, which led to a great career.

Q: What are you involved with at this time?

A: In my work life, I'm the sole electrical engineer for a design team that designs Coast Guard facilities. I design solar systems for offshore lighthouses and mobilize to hurricane-ravaged areas each year during hurricane season to provide engineering and logistical support for Coast Guard assets. And at home, I married my college sweetheart (from UMass) and we have two children (daughter Sarah is 8 yrs old & son Stefan is 8 months old). I'm always involved in working on my 1800's Victorian home, or off scuba diving around Cape Ann or sneaking in a round of golf. I'm also the President of The Coast Guard Investment Club, which is a group of ten people I work with, who pool their money to buy stocks.

Q: Can you compare the "old" you to the "new" you?

A: The old me didn't have back problems and the new me does. The old me was looking towards finding my niche in life and the new me has found that niche, a good paying job with great benefits and a wonderful family.

Q: What are your long-term plans?

A: To complete at least another 5 years in the federal government which will give me twenty years (includes my military service). I also have an interest in writing fiction and possibly producing a movie (I have a friend who is a movie producer...check out the movie Pi). That is my passion which I don't have time for right now.

Bonnie Chou

I began my Tufts journey as a R.E.A.L student in the spring of 2003. At that time, I had only been in the United States for just a little over two years. My English vocabulary did not exceed a thousand words and my English writing could not be longer than a short paragraph. Yet I expressed my strong will to study diligently and perform well. I was thus given the opportunity to study in one of the most celebrated colleges in the world, Tufts University, thanks to the R.E.A.L. program.

If it were not for the R.E.A.L program, I would never have had a chance to study in such a prestigious American university. When I first came to this country from Shanghai, China, I discovered that it is extremely difficult to enter into a selective college as an undergraduate. I had not attended a high school in the United States and I also carry credits from a foreign university that does not use English as its primary teaching language. This must have complicated my application to many other universities in the United States, simply because I do not fit into the proto-type of a transfer student. So I have to say, before I continue with my own experience, that R.E.A.L. is truly a pioneer program that opens a door for people over 25 years old with unique cultural and educational backgrounds. As a new immigrant, enrolling into Tufts University certainly means being fortunate means a twist of fate and means family honor. I still vividly remember how excited I was when I received the acceptance letter from Tufts. I phoned my parents overseas right away and we all sounded very emotional. That was a sleepless night for me, for my husband, and for my parents.

From spring of 2003 to spring of 2005, my undergraduate experience at Tufts University was enriched, fruitful and thus unforgettable, thanks to the R.E.A.L united community. If you think you have received an acceptance letter from Tufts and that is it, you are definitely wrong. That is just the beginning. From the welcoming dinner to "lunch with your favorite professors", from the R.E.A.L seminar (which is a great way to help us to quickly adapt into a competitive studying environment) to the R.E.A.L lounge, I was often amazed at how thoughtful this program is, and how much academic resource and attention we can obtain. I often asked myself, how can I not do well with all this support?

In the summer of 2004, I applied for the Tufts Summer Scholar program and was selected as one of that year's Summer Scholars, funded by the provost. As a Summer Scholar, I worked on a research-based software enhancement project, under the supervision of a professor from the Computer Science department. After three months of hard work, my mentor-professor and I presented our work After graduation, I was able to quickly find a software-related job because of this unique experience.

And I was never alone on the path to academic achievement. You would think that sometimes being over 25 years old and still studying among all young and fresh college undergraduates would be strange and psychologically not comfortable, and then you are wrong again. From day one at Tufts, I was introduced to and soon acquainted to my life long friend Eri Takashima. Later I got to know more and more R.E.A.L students from R.E.A.L activities, classrooms and the R.E.A.L lounge, where we could share our secrets of how to succeed in academic study. We encouraged each other to do better and we cherished each other's every little achievement. Until today, I am still actively in contact with quite a few people from the R.E.A.L program; they are my friends and they are my assets.

From the depths of my heart, I am so thankful that there was such a wonderful opportunity for me. It changed my life. As a Tufts graduate, I am privileged in finding jobs, and maybe in pursuing higher education in the near future. In 2003, a former R.E.A.L graduate custom-made golden star-shaped pins for each R.E.A.L student. The story that accompanied the starfish pin told of getting a "second chance." That's what the R.E.A.L. program has given so many.

David Kuo

After working for several years, I decided to go back to school and finish my undergraduate degree; however, I felt that I needed to find a school that understands the difficulties of adult learners returning to school. I spent countless hours doing research and talking to friends and relatives. I finally chose the R.E.A.L. program because it offered the most supportive program and individual attention. Some of us have not been in school for decades and it is hard to adjust to this new environment while taking care of family and holding down a job.

·For me, the first semester was the most important time of my life at Tufts. One of the most important lessons I learned was time management. At first it was hard to follow a schedule and get everything done with my new responsibilities. I learned to use my time wisely and after graduating from Tufts I still use the same techniques at work and am able to accomplish more. Not only did I master time management at Tufts, but I also gained confidence and a good foundation of knowledge in the fast-growing field of technology.

While at Tufts, I was fortunate to get elected as the Peer-Mentor Coordinator and then Vice-president of the Returning Students Organization (RSO) during my second and third years. This is a student-run organization that provides guidance and support to all R.E.A.L. students. My goal was to make connections among the new and current R.E.A.L. students. I was surprised to receive an overwhelming response from the students. I was happy to see how supportive they were and willing to find the time to help others when I know they have busy schedules.

With my technical background, my other goal was to create a website for the RSO, where new students, current students, and alumni can find

64   Diversity, Resiliency, Legacy

resources, post events, and share information. RSO staff positions have been created to keep up with technology and maintain the RSO website.

Tufts changed my outlook on life and my career path in more ways than I could have imagined. Not only did I receive a great education, but I also met some of my best friends. From time to time, I still stop by Carmichael Hall just to see what I can do to help make the R.E.A.L. lounge a better place, and I know I am not alone in doing this. The R.E.A.L. lounge is like my second home and the students and alumni are like family. I really appreciate the time and patient effort the program gave me during my years at Tufts.

Resiliency

R.E.A.L. students have come later to their education because of obstacles that the traditional-age student has not had to face. R.E.A.L. students have made it past many obstacles through a tiny window into a university education. Once at Tufts, they show resiliency again by rearranging their adult lives to the life of a university student and we have seen them persevere for the last thirty-five years.

Edita Zlatic

Q: I would like to start with your arrival to America.

A: I am originally from Bosnia. I was there during the war. After the war, my family moved to Germany where we stayed for five years. In Germany, they had this special law, rather a contract, saying that when the war was over, the Bosnian refugees had to either immigrate to another country or go back to Bosnia. It was not an option for my family to go back to Bosnia, so we decided to immigrate to the United States. At the time when we were supposed to go, my mom was not capable of traveling. The doctor said that she would not survive the flight. So, we decided that one of the sisters would come here, so I came in September 2000. The plan was that the rest of the family would come afterwards when my mom was capable of flying. However, Germany changed the laws saying that Bosnian refugees with post-traumatic stress disorders could stay. But I could not come back because I had already left Germany before the law changed.

Q: Can you tell me about the trip from Frankfurt, Germany, to wherever you were supposed to go?

A: I was supposed to fly to Phoenix, Arizona, but when we landed in Chicago (first U.S. stop), they took my passport and my documents. They said: "We just made short notice changes because we figured out that Phoenix was not the safest place for you to go." Originally, I should have gone to Los Angeles and stayed with my friend's sister, who would have been my sponsor. She would have paid for my school, she would have let me stay with her.

67

68   Diversity, Resiliency, Legacy

Everything would have been fine, but the organization in Germany denied it saying that because I am alone and criminality in Los Angeles is high, I should choose another city. And then I chose Phoenix, Arizona, because my other friend was there. I could stay with her family and go to school. My friend and her mom were waiting for me at the airport. But when I landed in Chicago, they (immigration) decided that Portland, Oregon was a much better place for me than Phoenix. They said it was for my security. I had this police guy making sure that I boarded the right plane to Portland.

Q: So, why didn't you fly from Portland to Arizona? Don't tell me that there were police officers waiting for you again?

A: There were other people waiting for me telling me "Welcome to America" and that I would actually not stay in Portland, Oregon but in Vancouver, Washington, which was just across the border from Oregon. I was exhausted. It was in the middle of the night. I was crying all the way from Chicago to Portland not even knowing where Portland is. And when I came there, there were these seven guys waiting for me. It was kind of scary. They put me with this host family and said that I would stay there and wait for my mom. When my mom comes, I can do whatever. But until she comes, I have to stay in this family and follow the rules. I was there for three months until I found out that my mom and my sisters were not coming. I had to endure this awful woman. She would make me cook and clean and take care of her kids. She did not want me to go to school. And almost every night she would bring the guys that I should meet because I could potentially marry them. I was 19 at the time.

Q: Then you got to know that your mom and family would not be coming because the German laws had changed.

A: Yes, they could stay. And it was actually better for them due to my mom's health problems. So I had to figure out what I was going to do. I got myself on line looking for schools. I was interested in international studies, security, conflict resolution and so on. I found a program at San Diego State University. The description was perfect for the things I wanted to study. I went to school part time and worked.

Q: What made you move from San Diego to Boston, and eventually to Tufts?

A: In San Diego, I met my boyfriend Jon. I was trying to get my life under control so I would not just be this working machine. I was living in this beautiful city for over a year and did not manage to go to the beach once. I could not go on like this, especially since I like the outdoors so much. Some time after I met Jon, he was accepted to MIT graduate school in Boston. He asked me to come with him. So, I decided to come here with him and look for a school. Boston has so many schools. I already knew about Tufts then. The Peace and Justice department was something that was really calling me. But I thought that there was no way I could pass the SAT with my English skills. I had to prepare myself for the high academic level at Tufts.

So, I ended up going to Fisher College, a junior college, for a year improving my English. I was there for three semesters when I decided to email professor Paul Joseph at Tufts. And I told him that this was my dream that I would like to do and that I would like to meet with him. And he said: "Sure, come on over. Let's talk." And we talked. It was supposed to be a half an hour talk and it ended up being a three-hour conversation. Mainly me talking about my life, things that I am interested in, things I want to do, things I did.

And then came the financial part of going to Tufts. I told him that there is no way I can afford it, it is too much. I had no financial support from anybody but the things I could do myself. And he said: " Another option would be … you are a little bit young for the program, but since you have so many experiences you might qualify to go to the R.E.A.L. program." I thought: "R.E.A.L. program? What is that?" And he picked up the phone while we were talking and called Dean Herbert. He left her a message and sent an email. She emailed me saying that we should meet. When I came to see her, she was so nice and sweet. So friendly. Everybody else, I am sure, who met with Dean Herbert, had this excellent experience. I felt really welcome. She asked me which schools I am applying for and I told her that it was Tufts and Harvard. And both Dean Herbert and Professor Joseph said that I should come to Tufts. It is a much better school for me.

Q: Why did you choose Tufts?

A: I love pretty much everything about it, especially because it is international. There is such a diverse student body here. People come from all possible backgrounds, different cultures, different languages. I love my classes. We are all there listening to the professor's lecture, later the discussion is opened up and everybody brings in something from a completely different perspective

70   Diversity, Resiliency, Legacy

that I have never thought about. I always come out learning something even more from my co-students than my professors. It is really an enriching experience. I like the fact that professors are there for you. They will always take their time to meet with you. Even if they are busy, they will squeeze you in somehow. Even if it is just emails, they are still communicating with you. They are interested to hear where you are going, what you want to do. And the campus is so beautiful with a warm atmosphere on it. I have no problems getting in touch with the younger students and hanging out with them. I think it is a great exchange with them. We have the book-smarts, and then we have the life-smarts meeting together.

Q: I know another thing about you. You just became an American a couple of months ago. How does it feel?

A: Excellent. It was a wonderful experience. Especially after all the struggle being a refugee in Germany, and always being a second-class citizen, not having the same rights. That bugged me a lot. But coming here to the United States, it was like a new beginning. New hope that things can be done. Right now, the sky is my only limit. It's a nice feeling that I can do pretty much anything that any other American can do. The ceremony itself was remarkable. There were over two thousand people saying the oath. It was a huge melting pot right there. And the judge said that we are coming from different countries bringing our traditions that we should not leave behind because we are citizens of this country. This is what makes this country what it is. There are good people, and good people are going to make good changes. Hopefully.

Q: What are your plans for after your graduation?

A: I am hoping to go to Egypt for a year to improve my Arabic. My aim is to be absolutely fluent in Arabic and hopefully speak the Egyptian dialect. After I come back, I will probably work for a year or two in the private sector or governmental, or non-governmental institutions getting experience of the real life. Later, I want to come back to academia and get my master's. Maybe here at Fletcher in law and diplomacy. Or maybe a Ph.D..

Sue Meaney

Q: Sue, can you please describe for me a day in your life prior to deciding to go back to college?

A: There are so many stages of my life before that. I can tell you that none of them were really fulfilling days. I was either going to work to do a job and coming home unfulfilled, or dealing with time when I was not working. Right before I decided to go back to school, I was in a program where I had to write down all of my jobs. I did it all – selling ice cream to driving limos, to being a manager at Fidelity Investments at the age of 17. From as high as you can go to as low as you can go. And nothing lasted, nothing worked. I was 26 years old at that time, when I realized that I was not able to keep a job. Nothing kept my interest. I did not have a specific direction or purpose to my life.

Q: When did you decide to go back to college?

A: I always wanted to go back. I did the leave-and-go-back routine a lot. I would always try to go back to school thinking that it would fix whatever was wrong with my life. When I was 25, I finally realized that I really needed to make a major change. I entered into a program; actually it was a detox program. I decided to do something positive with my life. To sit down and finish something. Up to that point, I had never finished what I started. After two years working hard to find out who I really was and being honest with myself, I decided to take some classes. Actually, I wanted to be a writer. I took a couple of classes at North Shore Community College where I realized that I had to take a science class. I took chemistry, and I LOVED it. I was taking poetry and chemistry and could not decide between the two. By my second semester at North Shore I was in the honors program, Phi Theta Kappa and all that. The woman who was heading the honors program pulled me into her office one day and said, "You don't belong here." I thought, "What did I do?" But she set an interview with Dean Herbert at Tufts University. I would have never thought that Tufts would be a place where I belong. You have to know that I come from a large Irish Catholic family, low middle class. There wasn't any money, ... so, school was not an option. I needed to get a job. But the director of the honors program sent me to Tufts.

Q: Are you the first from your family to have a college degree?

A: I have an older sister who went to Salem State for teaching. She is a teacher now. Out of eight of us, she went to Salem State and then no one else went to college. Until me.

Q: Would you say that your family supported you to go to college? What did your parents think?

A: I think that they wanted me to get a job. So, they were hesitant and supportive at the same time. But you know, I was never taught to reach for my dreams. In my house, it was important to survive.

Q: So, after walking out of Dean Herbert's office you could enroll at Tufts.

A: I could take two courses and if I got a B or better, I could matriculate to be a full-time student. And it was.... I mean, I walked in and this woman looked at me, and no one else in my life had ever done that before, and just believed in me. I never had that feeling before. ... I am going to cry. She took some of the things deep down inside me and pulled them out. Looked at them, saw them, gave them back to me. She really gave me a sense of "maybe I can actually do something." I never felt that supported before. That was brand new.

It was exciting and overwhelming. I would drive to school and would sit in the parking lot and cry my eyes out. Then turn around and go home waiting for the phone call for someone to say: "I am sorry. We didn't mean you. You can't come here. That was a mistake." It got easier later. From where my life is now to where it was ten years ago ... it's night and day. But it started when I passed organic chemistry. I started to take some English classes. I felt really comfortable there. I remember when I first started school. Came out of the shower, did the hair, put on my make up and got dressed. And then by the

Jean Herbert and Tina Marie Johnson　　73

end, you are lucky if you are rolling into class in your pajamas. But in the beginning I felt scared to death. Here I am sitting in organic chemistry, you know, here is this little girl from Revere, a recovering drug addict, 26 years old, and I felt like a fake. I was scared that people would find out that I don't belong here.

Q: What was your major?

A: I wanted to double major in everything. I wanted to take a million classes. I majored in chemistry and English at Tufts. I had to take some summer classes as well. I had to cram in all of the chemistry and poetry classes.

Q: How was the R.E.A.L. program for you?

A: I loved it. It kept me sane. I still have my journal. And sometimes I read it. I went through some tough times before I was enrolled in school, and the R.E.A.L. program helped me to get through it. I lost my brother-in-law due to an accident; I lost one of my dogs from heart failure. Being in the R.E.A.L. program, having a journal, and writing things down kept me connected to everyone there.

Q: How were your relationships with the professors?

A: Definitely good, especially Deborah Digges in the English department. I took all of her classes. She was great. And Mary Shultz in the chemistry department. Actually, I did a project and published the research when I was a junior. I brought my research to Mary Schultz and she brought my research to the other professors, to her seminar in California and everyone told her to go further with this. She gave me the lab time. So, in my spare time, I would be in the chemistry lab working on that project.

Q: What would you say is the biggest difference between a regular and a R.E.A.L. student?

A: I think that the biggest difference is that R.E.A.L. students know why they are there. They are there for a purpose to get the education and go a specific path. Whereas a regular student, I think, is there also for his or her social life. They are still developing mentally, socially, you know, being away from home for the first time. Not all of them but some of them. They may not necessarily see the value of the educational path. Whereas we have already done all that other stuff. We already figured out what we want to do.

74   Diversity, Resiliency, Legacy

Q: Tell me about your graduation.

A: I am so happy for my parents. They got to go to a R.E.A.L. college graduation. They were really, really proud. They finally realized that their fears were unwarranted. It was a very proud day for them. I think that was the biggest thing about that day. It was my parents, and how giddy they were with joy.

Q: What was your plan for after the graduation day?

A: I realized half way into my senior year that I wanted to go to vet school. I called the Tufts Veterinary School to find out what to do. And they said I needed some experience. When I worked at an animal clinic in Rockport, it just reinforced everything. I think that I grew up a lot that year. I gained a lot of confidence.

For a few months before the vet school started, I worked for World Rabies Vaccination Project. It is a wildlife rabies vaccination project at Cape Cod. I would go out at five o'clock in the morning, I would set traps the night before, and go in the morning and catch the wildlife, take blood samples, driving around in a pick-up truck and living in a tent. It was awesome.

Q: Earlier you mentioned that you went to Kenya. How did you get interested in Kenya?

A: I wrote a grant to the government to get money to do pediatric aids research. I went to work in an orphanage in Kenya. When I got there, the orphanage just said, "We changed our mind. You cannot work here." They were concerned about Western scientists coming over using and evaluating their people and not giving people credit. Which did happen, so I cannot blame them. But I ended up creating my own projects. I did two. I worked with thirty-six patients with HIV. They were what we call long-term-no-progressors. So, those were people who had HIV for a long time, but haven't got sick or progressed to AIDS. And the other half of the study was recording couples. Most of them were the same people, who were either in a relationship and not passing it on to their partner, or even having children and not passing it on to them. It involved staying in hospitals, in M.P. Shah Hospital in Nairobi. They gave me an office where I could interview people and do blood work on the people. I did blood work on their partners and their children and analyzed the different cells and stuff like that.

I went by myself. Everyone thought I was crazy. I created the entire project from nothing. It gave me such a great sense of what a person can do if they want to. And the people there … it was just amazing. You know, they have no pity for themselves. And you don't even know how bad it is. Including the people living without it (HIV). There was … destitution. It was dirty. No toilet. Sometimes I had water, sometimes I did not. I lived with armed guards. I got hijacked on a road by two guys with an AK 47. I mean, it's not like it was this glamour land but I understand that is how they survive.

After I came back, we took the data to people at MGH who do a lot of the same research and were looking at the same parameters. We were coming up with the same information, which was actually different from what was out there in the literature. The following summer, we pursued it even further with DNA.

Q: You got hijacked?

A: Yeah. I was on a road driving, which I was not supposed to do. I rented a car and taught myself to drive on the other side. And I was driving to meet some people that I had met. And I was lost. I was going up and down a couple of times on a road with no streetlights. That was a clear indication that this was a foreigner in a rental car. I was going down the road, and two guys came up from the side of the road. They were dressed in army fatigue, and they had an AK 47. I was scared. I thought this is it.

They started yelling at me, "You can't do that, you can't do that!" And I said, "Do what?" "You can't do that, you can't do that!" "What did I do?" And they said, "You can't do that. You are going to jail. You are never coming out." And I remembered something someone told me the first day I got there. And so I said, "Well, what would it take to make this better? How can I make this better?"

"Oh no, no. The judge is going to fine you."

"So if I give you the money and you give it to the judge, would that be ok?"

And they thought that was a good idea. So, I gave them the money. And then, one of them got into the car, sitting next to me with his gun kind of facing me and said, "I know you are lost. Where are you going? I will show

76 Diversity, Resiliency, Legacy

you." I told him. He showed me how to get where I was going. He got out of the car and walked all the way back to where we had been.

Q: What is next on your schedule?

A: It will be about rabies for a research project in Nepal. And I am looking into all the different carriers and the different species that are involved. Trying to get the project going similar to the project at Cape Cod. Basically, all of my projects involve infectious disease.

Q: What are you doing now?

A: I am a vet right now. I am going to do my internship next year (2006/2007) rather than last year. In the match program that is used for medical and veterinary students I was matched with my top choice. But unfortunately, my sister was really sick. I could not leave at that time when I was supposed to. My fourth year of vet school, a couple months into it, my sister (Katie) was diagnosed with cancer. So, I left school to take care of her. Basically, the rest of the fourth year I was taking care of her. I graduated in July rather than in May. And I lost my internship. I knew that potentially I could not get an internship because I was declined now. It was my fault. But they were really understanding and offered me the internship next year. So, I am going in June to California. The internship is in San Francisco, in the Bay Area. It is an emergency clinic. It will be great.

Q: How long will you stay?

A: One year. Right now, I have a temporary job. I am working for a hospital in Everett. We just opened a new corporate hospital. It is a veterinary practice, and until June, I will probably be staying in Everett. I love going to work and seeing people bringing in their pets, and we do anything for them – from ear swabs to cardiac problems. I love every minute when I am doing something that is important.

Q: What will happen when you finish your internship?

A: I have worked with a practitioner in Beverly. He is an older gentleman, a veterinarian, and he is going to retire. When I come back from San Francisco, I will work with him for a period of time until he decides to retire and I will taker over his practice.

Q: Wow. How do you feel about that?

A: Oh my god!!! I think, who are you? Are you that bad little girl? I was the one who used to go out and get drunk and smash cars. What do you mean that you are going to own a medical practice? I am very happy. Very proud.

Q: What would you say to a person who just mentioned to you that she/he is thinking about going back to college?

A: I would say absolutely. Follow your dreams. Don't let anything stop you. Don't worry about failing, don't worry about the money, don't worry about the logistics. I am over $200,000 in debt right now, but I am happy. And I could be 38 and be miserable. It's just money. I'll pay it off.

Derek Benoit

Q: Derek, could you please describe a day in your life prior to college?

A: Well, first I need to give you a little background. I grew up in Bristol, RI. I graduated high school in 1995, and I did go right into college. In fact, I didn't do poorly in high school and I was accepted to all four schools that I applied to. However, I didn't really know what I wanted to do, and my family was really strapped for money so college was a serious burden despite getting great financial aid. Freshman year (1996), I headed off to Western New England College, in Springfield, Mass. I enjoyed school and did fairly well, but I was trying to hold two jobs at the same time. The college raised tuition for the following year, so much so that I could not afford to go back. Therefore, my sophomore year I went to Rhode Island College. And began majoring in communications. I disliked the school and started to skip classes, and this ultimately led to me dropping out a year later. I remember making the decision to drop out, and though it was the right decision at the time, I never felt so low.

After that I did a lot to try and find my niche. I worked in retail, construction, insurance (studied and attained my licenses to sell life insurance), juvenile care, and finally made the move into the technical field in 2000. In January of 2001, I found myself laid off and down and out. I felt as though I had really hit bottom. I knew that it was time to make a serious change in my life. Instead of going on unemployment after the layoff in January, I went right back into interviews and found a job in Boston that would end up allowing me to facilitate my move back to school. When I took the job, I knew that

80   Diversity, Resiliency, Legacy

it would entail me moving to Boston, and I made a promise to myself that I would find a way to go back to school and the degree that I desperately wanted. I didn't know what that meant at the time – and I never dreamt that it would mean going to Tufts.

When I moved to Boston and started the new job I enrolled at Bunker Hill Community College and met some really incredible faculty and staff there that gave me a newfound belief in my abilities and I did really well in school for the first time in my life. It was then that I realized that my dreams could become realities with the right combination of motivation and energy.

Q: Was your family supportive?

A: Yes. I am the first in my family to go to college, so I am not sure that anyone in my family really understands the importance of education, or my desire to attain it. Friends were great though.

Q: How did you hear about the Tufts R.E.A.L. program and why did you decide to apply?

A: At Bunker Hill Community College I attended the orientation session, and I remember that very first day that they said that their graduates have gone on to Bentley, UMass, and "even" Tufts. That planted the seed in my head to learn more. I was living in Somerville and I remember the jealousy of being stuck at a traffic light one afternoon and seeing a Tufts University sticker on the back of the car in front of me. I remember saying to myself..."what I wouldn't give to be able to go there."

Q: Was your decision to come to Tufts a difficult one?

A: EXTREMELY difficult. While at BHCC I decided that I wanted to fulfill my dream of being a car designer. I started researching different schools, and trying to determine the best road to get me to where I wanted to go. The Harvard of car design schools is in Detroit. I went out to Detroit and talked to a counselor at the school. I received a conditional acceptance pending the review of my portfolio. Well right around this same time I learned about engineering psychology, and how that played a huge role in any type of design. I did some more research and found out that Tufts offered one of the few undergraduate programs in ENP in the country. I loved Boston so it all seemed to make sense to apply.

Q: How was your first semester?

A: I remember that my first class was a writing class and it was at night. I remember walking out of class and it was dark out, and the campus is gorgeous, as you know – but at night it is especially calming. I remember thinking that I was so lucky to be where I was. I have never felt more appreciative in my life. It was hard - VERY hard, but so rewarding at the same time. I worked full-time through my entire 3 years at Tufts and it was an incredibly difficult workload.

Q: What was your experience with Tufts professors?

A: Mostly positive. I had one math professor that I thought was a bit pompous. However, my next math professor was the best teacher that I have ever had – and I can say that about almost every other Tufts professor that I had; they are incredible.

Q: Were you involved in any research? Clubs?

A: Since I worked full-time and took 5 classes a semester, there really was not any time for much else. I wish I could have done it differently, but it was the only way I could make it work. I feel like I missed out on a lot, but it was still an amazing experience.

Q: What were your plans, your thoughts during your last semester at Tufts? About a job? Grad school?

A: As I said in my first response, I moved to Boston to pursue a job. That job became more and more challenging as my years at Tufts went on. My job was the other piece that made going to Tufts a possibility. They were so flexible with my schedule. There were days that I literally went back and forth from work to school 3 times in a day. It was exhausting. However, by my final semester they had promoted me to a management position so I was really stressed. I decided to focus on my career after I graduated and see where it leads me. The company I work for is in a huge growth spurt so it is a very exciting, and financially fulfilling position. I think that in a few years

82   Diversity, Resiliency, Legacy

I may continue my pursuit of becoming a car designer. Tufts has gotten me half-way there.

Q: Did you have any difficulties at Tufts?

A: Of course I did. For me, again due to my full-time workload, it was always stressful trying to find time to fit all of my required classes in my schedule and have time to work. Math was also a serious struggle for me. It was also difficult to not have time to spend with classmates or other R.E.A.L. students. That support group was missing from my life, and it really took its toll on me by the end. It is hard enough being an older student and not fitting in – but combining that feeling with loneliness on campus made it that much harder.

Q: How did Tufts R.E.A.L. program change your family's life?

A: The R.E.A.L. program gave me the confidence that I needed. It gave me hope. It gave me a newfound passion for learning. It completely changed my life. But I think most importantly, and I cannot stress this enough, the R.E.A.L. program provided for me a chance to start again. When you're in the position that I was in – and so many other R.E.A.L. students can attest to this – you feel like you're in a hole somewhere looking up. Even though you can see the world up there at the top, it feels like you can't get there. You can hear what's going on and it sounds really exciting, but you're not there. Getting accepted to Tufts is like someone throwing down a rope. It's an opportunity. They don't come down there and lift you out of the hole – you have to climb. It's hard work. It's really hard work. But you take hold of that rope and you start climbing, and climbing, and climbing. Soon you realize that the world is getting closer and closer into view. Next thing you know, you're out of the hole and dusting yourself off. You can see the sun again, and everything is beautiful – so much more beautiful than you ever imagined. But it takes someone reaching out and empowering you with a way out. The R.E.A.L. program, is what makes it possible. At its most basic level – it's about humanity – people helping people. Isn't that what education is supposed to be all about? This program changed my life, and the lives of every single other R.E.A.L. student that I have spoken to.

Q: What are you involved in at this time?

A: Work, work, and more work

Q: Can you compare the "old" you to the "new" you?

A: Honestly – I cannot. I cannot compare that lost, confused, disorganized Derek from my past. That person is unrecognizable to me. Like I said, I have started over. I am a new person. I am the person that I always wanted to be.

Q: What are your long-term plans?

A: The world is in my hands. Right now I am focused on doing well at work, and potentially going to design school in Detroit in a few years. Other than that I would love to get married and have children some day. Maybe own a little cabin on a lake up in Maine somewhere. The best part is that I now know (thanks to Tufts) that I can do whatever I want to do! Thanks so much Dean Herbert. You have made such an amazing impact on more people than I think you know. Thank you for throwing down the rope.

Theresa Maggiore

The R.E.A.L. program came at an extreme turning point in my life. In the fall before my 39th birthday, I decided I was going to finally do what I had always dreamed of and get a bachelor's degree. When I graduated from high school in 1974, my guidance counselor told me I would not be able to go to medical school like I wanted. In effect, he told me – girls can't do that and besides you're from a poor background where will you get the money? This statement burned in me for years and I was determined to prove him wrong.

After several successful careers, I decided to look into returning to school to extend the associate's degree I held into a bachelor's degree, but I was afraid. Would I be too old, not smart enough? Self doubt pervaded and I opted for a class at a community college. Once there, I found out I was none of those, and my confidence bolstered. I found myself inquiring about Tufts University and was put in touch with the R.E.A.L. program. In the same week I received an acceptance letter from Tufts, I also received notification I was going to have a baby. Now, what to do? I had a job, two children at home and one on the way. My husband convinced me we could make it work and that I should pursue my dream

In September of 1995, at 7 months pregnant, I began my R.E.A.L. life journey. Sitting in class behind "my desk" (actually, two desks strategically placed to fit my growing girth), with students who could have been my child, could have sent me home crying, but the encouragement I got from the faculty, other R.E.A.L. students, and the young students in class was remarkable. They pulled me along and valued my life experiences in class discussion. I soon found myself forgetting my size and became totally engrossed in learning.

When November came, I delivered our third beautiful boy, who was born deaf and blind. My grief was overwhelming at first. But continued contact with faculty and the friends I had made, along with the support of a loving family, made me realize this was just one more challenge that life had brought me. I had learned in the last few months that I could survive and thrive under challenge. My cousin told me, God gave him to you, because he knows you are strong enough to give him a good life. So my husband and I took control, researched the right contacts and information, and were determined to make everything work.

While we tackled our son's first year of life, the faculty, students and staff supported me to continue on with classes. They provided a shoulder to cry on, an ear to listen and a temporary escape, that allowed me to go back to the tasks of caring for my family with renewed vigor.

I am proud to say that today our son who was born during my time in the R.E.A.L. program is a happy 10 year-old. His hearing is normal (due to surgery) and he is able to see with low vision out of one eye. This has not hampered him in any way. He plays hockey and soccer, is a star actor in all school plays, is goalie for his two older brothers in a game of street hockey and just hosted a 7-boy sleepover for his birthday. The courage that I gained in the R.E.A.L. program was conveyed to him from birth, that no matter what it is, if you want it bad enough, it will come true.

When I walked across that stage in 1998 to complete my long-awaited dream and accept my diploma, I knew I was not finished. I went on to get a master's degree in education at UMass Boston. Today I am a Teacher of the Visually Impaired in the Boston Public Schools, helping children each day to recognize their dreams and providing them with the tools to make it come true. They will never hear from me "you can't do that" for I know that a dream delayed can be a dream realized no matter how long or how challenging with the right support.

Michelle Botus

One month after graduating from high school, I gave birth to my first child. Needless to say at that time my priority was not to continue my education, but instead, to raise my daughter. One year later, I got married and took on the role of wife and mother. I spent the next twenty years taking care of my husband, my first daughter and the three other children that came after her.

For the past three years, I've been working at a substance abuse program for pregnant and nursing women. I enjoy my work in the house and I feel that my presence there has been a positive influence on the women. In the three years that I've been at my job, I have been encouraging the women there to continue their education. So far, four of the clients have enrolled and are attending classes at Bunker Hill Community College.

I feel that it is important for me to share that I am a survivor of domestic violence. On May 1, 2001 my husband of twenty years tried to kill me. He was arrested and I fled my home and everything I owned. I brought with me only my most valuable assets: my children. At that time, my children were 19, 12, 4, and 4 months old. For my safety, I was placed in a domestic violence safe-house for three months. While at the shelter, I decided that I needed to go back to school and earn a degree to provide a better future for my children. When I started attending classes at Bunker Hill Community College I was still homeless, although no longer at the domestic violence safe house, but at a family shelter. Thanks to the programs and services that had been made available to me at the shelter, I became a One Family Scholar.

88   Diversity, Resiliency, Legacy

For the last two years I have been working with the One Family Scholarship Program to help educate the public on issues around family homelessness. While I was living in the shelter I dreamed of having a home for my family. I am no longer homeless, but now I have a new dream. My dream is to develop a program for survivors of domestic violence. My program will have a heavy emphasis on higher education because I believe that empowerment comes through education and empowerment and abuse cannot share a home.

Laura M.

Q: Laura, could you please describe for me a day in your life before you started school again?

A: Well, I worked full time and took classes part time. It was pretty chaotic. I had attended a junior college for three years and had an associate's degree in communications. I felt that this was not enough education and wanted to go back to complete my bachelor's. I was working at Harvard at the time and my career advancement was limited. They were pretty open about it at Harvard but without a bachelor's degree I would not be able to pursue some other job opportunities. Since I was working at Harvard, I was also taking classes there and kind of packaged myself to get ready to apply to the R.E.A.L. program.

Q: Did you decide to go back because of your job?

A: Because of my job, and because I always wanted to complete my bachelor's degree. I never intended to drop out of school. But I had to due to financial reasons. I always wanted to finish my bachelor's degree.

Q: Why did you then decide on the R.E.A.L. program?

A: I liked the idea of being in a community of adult learners. Since I went back at the age of 27, I did not feel that I fit into the community of 18-22 year olds. It also appealed to me to be a part of a program that offered a higher level of intimacy one on one with the professors due to my experience from Harvard.

90   Diversity, Resiliency, Legacy

I liked the more professional approach in the R.E.A.L. program. It wasn't just transferring into any school; I felt like I would not be an isolated student.

Q: Why did you choose to study US History?

A: Well, it appealed to me at the time. Prior to that I spent some time with my grandparents who both lived during the Great Depression; they both came from different countries and so were first generation immigrants and carved a life here for themselves. They used to tell me stories about their families, the old countries and about the transition; what it felt like to be an American and what their process of naturalization was like. I just became interested in history, gradually taking more and more classes. I wanted to learn about the social and human perspective; how people overcome difficulties; why people move to a completely different country. For me it was about what makes people pursue their passions and make their life better, the individual experiences.

Q: How did you find out about the R.E.A.L. program? Was it supportive for you and if yes, how?

A: I found out about it through a woman with whom I had worked in the admission office at Harvard. She was my boss and the director of admissions. She heard about the R.E.A.L. program and told me about it. She said that it is a nice program for older students like myself. I don't think that she knew anybody who went through it but she was aware of it as an admittance counselor. And how did I like the program? It was fantastic. It was nice to have a group of people who like me had to quit their jobs, really good jobs, and go back to school to finish something that they wanted to do. It was really inspiring. We were all in different programs at Tufts, each doing his or her own thing. It was really interesting to be around people who just sort of wanted to finish their degree and be in an academic environment with other older students and younger students. It made the re-entry and the process of finishing much easier, more comfortable. It offered a resource that helped me to cope with the transition.

Q: What kind of resources?

A: Friendship, social and also financial. Study groups. My problem was that I had to take a calculus class and I hadn't had math since I was a junior in high school which was about ten years prior. I went to my first class and was kind of horrified because I was in school with kids who had a lot of recent math, were involved with math methods that were more active than the methods when I took mathematics. We were standing in line after class to speak to the teacher and I noticed that there was another girl who was also standing in line. And I just approached her saying: "Look, I need extra help already and it is only day one." (Laughs). As an older student I just started the talking. She ended up being my roommate for the next two years and is still a good friend of mine. We both agreed how much we were in misery and how much we are going to dread this class. We studied together, we studied for tests together and we would quiz each other. It made the whole experience more enjoyable.

Q: Did you participate in any kind of clubs, organizations, study abroad, or other activities at Tufts?

A: No, I didn't. I didn't really have the money to study abroad. I didn't participate in any clubs because I really felt that it was for the younger kids. Also, as an older student, I could go out and drink with my friends. I had been living in Davis Square for over ten years by then and had my friends outside of school. So, I really did not use any of the social resources on the campus because I already had established relationships. But I did hang out with the R.E.A.L. students in the program. We had BBQs, parties, cocktails, you know, the usual.

Q: Did you have to work while you were at Tufts?

A: Oh yeah. I had a part time job the year around. And when I was on vacation I worked full-time.

Q: Where did you work?

A: I stayed at Harvard. I went back as an hourly contractor. I was a receptionist basically for the admission office where I worked before I went back to school. I asked them if I could help out in any way and they agreed. Since their usual pool of work-study students would often be absent during the summer and I was on vacation, it was really easy for me to go back and fill in the blanks that the students left.

Q: After your graduation, did you pursue graduate school or did you head to the workforce?

A: After graduation I went to work for a law firm as a paralegal. It was a small firm in town called Redmond. I worked there for four years.

92   Diversity, Resiliency, Legacy

Q: How did you enjoy the work there?

A: I went there with the intention to go to law school. Being a paralegal for a year also helped me to get on my feet financially. I also wanted to get a better understanding of what the law practice was like. But during a very short period of time it was clear to me that I didn't want to study the law. So, after four years, I took four months off and decided that I wanted a career in marketing. I got a job as a marketing coordinator in software company.

Q: And how did you like this job?

A: I liked it a lot. It was really exciting even though it was not an easy job. They did not have much money as a startup and so we had to do a lot of different things. Talk to attorneys, plug in phones, screw in light bulbs, do marketing, go to trade shows, work with sales people, talk to customers, whatever needed to be done.

After the startup software company, I went to a publicly owned company in Lexington that makes children's shoes. I took a job there as an assistant marketing manager and stayed there for a year. After this I moved to another privately held company, a family owned company, and was a marketing manager in product marketing there. From there I went to a public television station and was the marketing manager for educational production working on a privately funded project. For the last year I have been working at Gillette.

Q: What is the role that Tufts played in your life?

A: That is funny. I did some coaching work a while back and one of my coaches asked me what my three greatest achievements were. And the first one that came to me was going back to school. So, I consider going back to school and being part of the R.E.A.L. program one of my greatest achievements. Mainly because it would have been so easy for me to drop out of college and go be a bartender making a fair amount of money for the rest of my life.

Tufts is a great school and I never thought that I would be able to get in there. The atmosphere was so inspiring. I always wanted to model that kind of passion and be really happy and excited about whatever I was doing. My experience at Tufts gave me the foundation for going out and pursuing what I wanted to pursue. And also the competency to just go and do it.

Q: How would you describe your interaction with the professors?

A: It was great. As a matter of fact, I came across my professor Gerry Gill in the history department while I worked on a project with the television station. He was one of the advisors on the project. It was nice to see him again. My relationship with the professors was great. I had a lot of respect for them and they had a lot of respect for me as an older student.

George

Before I learned that something called the R.E.A.L. Program existed, I thought I was going to have to live the rest of my life with the stark reality that I had totally screwed up my undergraduate career and had destroyed any chance I would ever have for entering graduate school. I mean, let's be honest, it's pretty rare in life that one gets a second chance to essentially return to the past to try and do something over the way he wished he had done it in the first place. Tufts' R.E.A.L. Program was like a gate through which I was able to walk back into my past and amend the errors I made when I was too undisciplined to know what I was really doing. Let me illustrate.

When I entered college back in the early 90's, my original intension was to excel academically and to prepare myself for a professional degree. Well, that didn't happen. My pitfall was nothing spectacular or unheard of. I simply traded these goals for the fleeting excitement of the undergraduate party scene. I treated my well-ranked university more like a nightclub (with a $10,000 cover charge!) than as a place for higher learning. Not surprisingly, I massacred my academic record and was invited, eventually, to withdraw.

For the next several years, I worked as a clerk in a bookstore, which was the only job I could land at the time, in order to begin paying back my squandered college loans. As I mopped floors and shelved books, I tortured myself daily with the knowledge that my peers were progressing toward their careers in business, medicine, and law, while I faced the fact that I was mired in my current situation. I didn't know where to begin to look to redeem myself academically. Getting a degree on-line, from my local community college, or a school with an open-enrollment program wouldn't make me an attractive candidate to graduate schools that naturally seek out students from the more

95

96   Diversity, Resiliency, Legacy

competitive universities. Yet with my checkered past academic record, where could I go? I could see no way out of this pit. It was a dark time.

I forget exactly how I came to learn about the R.E.A.L. program, but when I stopped by Tufts to learn more about it, I was most impressed by the fact that I was assured that I would once again have a chance to get what I had believed would never again be within my grasp—a bona-fide degree from a top-ranked university. I had investigated plenty of options for completing my undergraduate education in the New England area, but Tufts' R.E.A.L. program was the only one offering an opportunity to obtain something more than just an extension-school adjunct degree.

Unlike other institutions that have open-enrollment programs available to the community at large, admission to the Tufts R.E.A.L. program is a competitive one. It involved a selective enrollment process complete with an application procedure that required a personal essay, recommendations, standardized test scores, my high school transcript, and an interview. In short, it felt like I was applying to college all over again from the beginning. Tufts was offering me a chance at a fresh start. And I was assured that, if accepted, I would be granted a place alongside the other, more traditional students, in the next matriculating class with all of us eligible for a regular Tufts degree.

The rewards I received from Tufts are immense. Let me tell you about a few. Not only was I able to challenge myself anew in a highly competitive academic environment, but also, I am grateful that I was given the chance to erase the regrets that I carried for not having seized certain opportunities when I was an undergrad years before. For example, whenever I returned home to Boston on break from my former school, I would watch the scullers rowing along the Charles. I always wanted to have the experience of being part of a crew team and competing in a regatta, and I often kicked myself for not having had the discipline to join. Clearly, my former party-oriented lifestyle was incompatible with getting up between 4:30 or 5:00 in the morning, being on the river by 6:00, and as their motto says, "Doing more before 8:00 than some people do all day". Through the R.E.A.L. program, I was able to erase that particular regret from my life. For two years I rowed on Tufts' crew team, competing in the Head-of-the-Charles and other regattas around New England. I'll confess, however, it was more difficult than I anticipated for a guy in his 30's rowing with younger men in their late teens and early 20's, trying to keep up, but it was a challenge well worth my undertaking.

Yet another regret that I was able to eradicate because of the R.E.A.L. program ultimately, and unexpectedly, led me to the satisfying career path I am on today. I had always been envious of my peers who managed to organize their course of study so they could go abroad for a semester or for a year. I noticed that when they returned, they were changed in ways I admired. They

Jean Herbert and Tina Marie Johnson 97

appeared more worldly, more knowledgeable, and more appreciative of so many things. They had added a certain kind of breadth and depth to their education that I desired.

At Tufts, one particular graduation requirement led me to perhaps the most fulfilling experience I have undertaken to date. I chose to study the Japanese language, and learned through the department about an opportunity to work in Japan as an English teacher. Now, I'll be honest—pursuing a career in education was not part of my original undergraduate agenda. I saw this merely as a chance to have that international experience I so longed for. Nevertheless, I was determined to ensure I would get the most out of it. I do know that the more I learn about a subject, the more I can appreciate it. With this in mind, I structured a large part of my coursework around this goal. At Tufts, I was given the chance to study Japanese history, cinema, literature, poetry, music, culture, language, and their performing arts.

When I did eventually move to Japan for this teaching position, my preparation served me well. I found I was experiencing the culture on a level deeper than that of a mere tourist and was able to attain a level of immersion that left a lasting impression on me. Perhaps most significantly, however, is that I discovered teaching absolutely thrilled me. When I returned to the States after three years, I was fortunate enough, due in no small part to my teaching experience in Japan, to be hired by the Education Department at Harvard's Museum of Natural History, where I am working today. This spring, I expect to be working towards my master's degree in education here at Harvard.

Carrying regrets for past indiscretions is agonizing. So, too, is the feeling that there is no hope for redemption. Tufts not only gave me a rare chance to both amend my past and redeem myself, but also put me on a most enjoyable career path I might otherwise never have chosen. The R.E.A.L. program was an opportunity I cherish and one for which I will always be wholeheartedly grateful.

Amy (Scallon) Adolfo

Q: Amy, could you please tell me what you were doing before going to Tufts?

A: I was a student at Bunker Hill Community College and prior to that I was working full-time in Rhode Island as a care provider in a group home. After high school, I was certified as a nursing assistant. I knew that I wanted to work in health care. I was not really sure if I wanted to go to college and study medicine, so I received a certification as a nursing assistant and worked at a nursing home for a while. But I found out that that wasn't really what I wanted to do so I switched to the psychology world and worked as a care provider.

Q: How and why did you decide to move to Boston?

A: I knew that I wanted to return to school. I graduated high school in 1992, five years prior. I knew that Boston was the place I wanted to be and I knew that I needed to start at a community college. When I got there I really excelled in my coursework, and became involved in student activities and student government as well. Also, it was at that time that I found out about the R.E.A.L. program. I applied and interviewed with Dean Herbert. I remember getting the acceptance letter and being very excited. I never thought coming from a community college I would end up at a place like Tufts.

Q: How was your experience at Tufts?

100 Diversity, Resiliency, Legacy

A: Very positive. I was the president of the R.E.A.L. student group and I was able to go abroad to France. That was a good experience for me. I was only a few years older than the seniors. So I felt like I was an adult student with maybe more experience and more wisdom but I still could fit in with some of the undergraduate students. Plus I didn't have family obligations or children to care for so I was able to experience some of what the undergraduates were experiencing.

Q: What did you study in France?

A: Well, it was the Tufts' summer school in France, and I studied the Flowers of the Alps and also French. It was great.

Q: Did you have any support from your family?

A: I definitely had their emotional support. They were happy for me to be going back to school, but financially, not really. I had very little support. Sometimes they would help me to pay the rent but that is about it.

Q: How would you describe your life prior going back to college?

A: I would say average. I would go to work and have a job that really did not have any impact on the world around me. Unfulfilled. That is a good word. I wasn't challenged. I felt like I had more to give. I had a lot of potential but I wasn't doing anything with it. And when I was at Bunker Hill, it was very hectic because I was commuting to Boston from Providence. I would have my classes from 8 to 2 then I would go home and work a job from 3 to 11pm and the next day do it all again.

Q: That is amazing that you could do that commute like that and do really well at school at the same time.

A: Yeah. Luckily I had a job at a group home where the four men that I cared for went to bed at 8 o'clock. So between eight and eleven I could do my homework.

Q: Let's fast forward to graduation time. What were your plans afterwards?

A: I was accepted to the post-bacc program at Tufts. I wanted to continue with the program and go to medical school. That was the plan.

Jean Herbert and Tina Marie Johnson

Q: And is that what happened?

A: No, it is not. I started my first semester of chemistry but I couldn't afford to live in Boston anymore. I thought that I would be able to commute from Providence and do the post-bacc program but it wasn't working. I had to take out student loans on top of the student loans that I had to take out as an undergraduate. I took new loans, deferred the old ones and commuted but it really wasn't working out. And once when I was home I was looking through the Providence Journal and noticed a job at Brown University for a research assistant. I had taken a research class at Tufts that got me really interested in research so when I noticed this job at Brown and part of their benefits is that Brown pays for you to go to school, it was an opportunity I couldn't resist. It just made sense to me that I could do their community health program in Rhode Island where I could live for free with my family and not to have to take out more student loans.

Q: Has anything else happened in your life since graduation?

A: I got married a year ago in November. And I have an 8-month-old daughter now.

Sarah Mocas

The R.E.A.L. Program was my chance to get a great education. I remember applying to Tufts – I had very little money and didn't really believe that, even if I was accepted, I would be able to afford the school. On the other hand, I had nothing to lose in applying! It is still amazing to me that I was given that opportunity.

It's been a while, at least 20 years since I was at Tufts, but I can still remember being a bit on my own both in and out of school. My friends, who were all working, didn't have a clue how demanding school was for me, and my fellow students were immersed in the general flow of campus life. It didn't help that I was a computer science major and my classmates were mostly guys ten years my junior. I remember feeling a little like an old lady (I was only in my thirties!), sitting in the computer science lab late at night, furiously working on my programs, hoping to get all the bugs out before the midnight submission deadline. Fortunately, the R.E.A.L. director, several of my professors and friendships with other R.E.A.L. students carried me through.

Along with all the work, I clearly remember what a luxury it was to be able to learn. I was very conscious of this at the time. Of how amazing it was to think about Cantor's notions of infinite sets or learn about Asian aesthetics. This is the R.E.A.L. gift of the R.E.A.L. program – allowing people who are not prepared to jump straight from high school into college the pure luxury of learning.

The professors at Tufts inspired me to learn. I don't use the term "inspired" lightly. I was given a confidence in my intelligence and an understanding in the broader possibilities that were there for me. To make a long story short, I went on to get a Master's and Ph.D. in computer science from Northeastern University, and to become an Assistant Professor at Portland State University

104   Diversity, Resiliency, Legacy

(Portland, Oregon). I especially love counseling older students, passing on to them a broader sense of the possibilities in their lives.

Once again I'm setting off in a new direction. Not completely new since, at the core of it, I am learning about something that I love, and hopefully passing on in an inspired way. I am exploring video as a medium for expressing my long-term interests in Asian culture and specifically meditation practices. I am learning about video development, both writing narration and editing. My first effort combines an ancient Buddhist meditation practice, Chöd, and Asian art in a short documentary, Art of Chöd.

It's been an exciting twenty years since graduation and, without reservation, I can say that I've lived a life that was unimaginable before I attended Tufts.

Eric Erkenbrack

Believe it or not, immediately after high school, I had convinced myself that college was not for me. I thought life was as easy as going out into the world and finding a job. That was in 1998. By 2002, I had reversed my naïve decision. I had experienced a personal renaissance. I was voraciously reading works by great thinkers like Carl Sagan, Richard Dawkins, Plato, Nietzsche. These individuals were my personal teachers; and I learned much from them. In January 2003, I matriculated at Normandale Community College in Minnesota; suddenly, I had goals. I had steady jobs throughout that time-- working 45 hours a week and taking 5 courses a semester. I worked for a hotel, a casino, and a race track. This whole period in my life is a flash. I remember very little. What I do remember most is being accepted to Tufts. And I can honestly say that it made all the hustle-and-bustle worth it.

I came to Medford in the summer of 2005. I was given the opportunity--and what I thought to be an extraordinary one at that--to do ecology research over the summer prior to my matriculation. This is where I first came to know what it meant to be a Jumbo. Professor Colin Orians showed me first-hand what his job entailed and introduced me personally to all of the biology faculty members at Tufts. We regularly met to discuss problems in biology, experimental design, interpreting results, writing academic papers, etc.. That summer I learned what distinguishes a Tufts education: an intimate and nurturing learning environment. As the summer ended, I thought to myself that this couldn't be the norm; certainly this level of personal involvement couldn't possibly be maintained during the semester. But I was fortunately mistaken.

My experiences at Tufts are unique due to the extraordinary faculty. They take their time and guide you into problems. They are, however, not so quick to show you the solutions, rather they let you learn by confronting them and

106   Diversity, Resiliency, Legacy

struggling with them just long enough. What's more, it didn't take me long to realize that I had entered another academic stratum. The students were singularly clever and marked by a peculiar and persistent desire to learn. But as you are only as great as those people with whom you surround yourself, I greeted these individuals with enthusiasm. My first year at Tufts, having written a quality, full-length biology paper, achieved excellent grades, and made great friends, was a marked success. Nevertheless, I wasn't quite content with halting there.

Since Tufts offers some of the friendliest and most attractive opportunities to travel abroad of any college in the US, I decided it would be a great idea to spend a year in Germany. Keeping this in mind, I had applied to various scholarship programs in Germany, hoping to further beatify my experience there. These were mainly government-funded programs aimed at North American college students like 'Research Internships in Science and Engineering', 'University summer intensive language studies', and the 'Undergraduate research fellowship'. Much to my surprise, I received them all and consequently spent 15 months living and working in Germany. What's more, the flexibility to these programs allowed me to integrate them with Tufts-in-Tuebingen program abroad. And although I spent most of my time working in laboratories, I got to acquire an additional language while doing it. What I learned in Germany I will utilize for the rest of my life and can only be thought of as indispensable. Now I'm back at Tufts for one last go--the denouement of my undergraduate years. Reflecting on all of my pre-Tufts options, I can't unequivocally say that I wouldn't have taken a similar path at some other institution. (It's not even fair to say that it could have been any other way. After all, I am a philosophy major.) However, what I can assert is that my experience is unique, indelible, and unforgettable. Important decisions in your life--for example, which college to attend--certainly always seem to be hi-jacked by conditional statements--the 'what-ifs'. They will always surface here and there. But I certainly need not worry about such a statement clouding my reasoning about the value of coming to Tufts. In the end, the best compliment I can give Tufts is that I wouldn't want it any other way.

Peter Malkin

Q: Please tell me something about your life prior to deciding to go back to college.

A: I went to Brandeis for several years. For three years I was a physics major because my father was a physicist and I thought that this was a good thing to be. But I was miserable. So, I dropped out of there and I worked for three years. I worked at a company close to Burlington Mall. It was mainly robotics. Eventually I started to look into going back to school. I was trying to figure out where to go and a friend of mine told me to check out the R.E.A.L. program at Tufts. I went to talk to the dean about the program and it was great. It was a match.

Q: You said that you worked in robotics before you came to Tufts. What was your job?

A: My associates made electronic instruments like capacitors, stuff for missiles, and they needed to test these things before they sold them. My group built systems that tested things faster. It was better for the company to put the instruments into a big robotic handler than to have a lot of people sitting around in a room, holding little instruments. It was basically giving the company a little bit of an edge. The robotics was fun. It was controlling real stuff and getting to watch things happen.

Q: So, why did you decide to go back to college?

108 Diversity, Resiliency, Legacy

A: I think that I always wanted to go back but I was waiting until I was ready. I was always uptight about school and really intimidated by it. But when I went back, it was much more--I will use the term self-indulgent--because when you are at school at a later time, all the exercises become a way to learn, unlike work where you have to do something for someone else. And the teachers were not intimidating anymore.

Q: What did you major in at Tufts?

A: I majored in computer science. But I also met Professor George Smith, who taught logic. I had a free period and somebody told me to take this class and it was a blast. I ended up doing a kind of computer reasoning like artificial intelligence. But I really centered my classes around what Professor Smith was teaching.

I also did an independent project with Professor Smith and two computer science teachers. We were trying to do artificial intelligence using automatic reasoning. And it was also connected to other fields and not just straight computer science stuff, so that was nice.

Q: What did you do after graduation?

A: It turned out that my grades were really good and I was invited to apply for a fellowship. I applied for and received the ITT Fulbright Scholarship to Australia. That went really well. The fellowship was to work with a group in Australia doing automated reasoning using non-classical logic, another kind of logic than the one we had used in our project at Tufts. There was this great team at the international university and I got to work there for a year. Upon my return, I applied to graduate schools, but only master's programs because I really didn't want to go to school that much more. Especially since you need about five years for a Ph.D.. I was accepted to a program in Rhode Island. I got a master's degree in Computer Science there. I worked with a woman name Leola Morgenstern, who taught at Brown then, on automated reasoning again, which is what I did my master's thesis on. And the funny part is that now I work with her in the IBM research department. Her office is two doors down from mine.

Q: What is your exact job at IBM?

A: Originally I got hired into the robotics group, the artificial intelligence group. But what I have been doing the past two years are database systems

Jean Herbert and Tina Marie Johnson 109

allowing various kinds of programs to store or create data, fancy kinds of data. I also get to work on patents. About four years ago, I was made the master inventor. I get to come up with an idea and bring in different people and make it into a bigger idea and then we can patent it. IBM likes patents. It's fun. In some ways it's better than regular projects because you can finish a patent in less than half a year. Many other projects that I have been working on have been canceled along the way for some technical difficulties. But patents are like creative writing. It's a lot of fun to talk to people on different kinds of ideas. I enjoy that.

Q: What other things changed about your life after your graduation from Tufts and the R.E.A.L. program?

A: I think that it really changed. For one thing, I used to be terrified about writing papers. I was really terrified. In the patent process you need to get your ideas organized and thus it becomes a paper. It's actually writing a paper which is being judged by other people, the patent office and then again, and again. The whole Tufts experience gave me self-confidence.

Q: Would you do it again?

A: Absolutely. And I would have everyone else do it also. Because when you come back later on, you have a much different attitude, a much better attitude. You have more background about what everything means and where you might use it. I feel much less vulnerable than how I felt before. I would tell anyone to do it. And the program at Tufts is so wonderful. Professors like us because we ask questions and keep things lively. Tufts is a great university also. So, I would recommend it to anyone.

Stephanie Tusa

I still remember the day I phoned Tufts University deans' office to inquire about the undergraduate degree program; that day changed my life. I was so incredibly frustrated with the lack of response that I had received from other colleges and universities when I phoned to inquire about their full-time undergraduate programs. Although I had never taken my SATs, I had just completed my Associate's Degree in Business Management while working full-time, had been with my then current employer for 10 years and I had life experiences, yet nobody wanted to talk to me until I took my SATs. As a last ditch, effort – and a stretch – I phoned Tufts and Jean Herbert, Program Director for the R.E.A.L. program, happened to have answered the phone. I knew nothing of the program but she spoke of it at length and encouraged me to apply. After my formal interview and application process, I was accepted into the program.

If not for the R.E.A.L. program, I never would have been afforded the opportunity to complete my studies at such a highly respected university. As a lifelong Medford resident, I knew of the university's reputation and had dreamed of obtaining an education at such a prestigious institution; the program allowed me to achieve that dream, which opened up so many doors for me.

Upon graduation in 1999, I sought a position within a large, well-known organization that recruited at highly regarded universities such as Tufts. As an English major, I strengthened both my written and oral communication skills; skills that have become so important in a corporate environment. In addition, the combination of my prior corporate experience, along with my degree from Tufts, made me a more desirable hire. Having continued my education on a full-time basis demonstrated a commitment that brings forth a sense of hard work and dedication that is so important to employers.

112   Diversity, Resiliency, Legacy

I left the above to accept a position with another well-known organization, American Express Financial Advisors. In May 2000, I was hired as the Operations Manager for their largest and most successful financial advisor office. In October 2005, American Express spun off the Financial Advisor Group and I continue to work for the new company, Ameriprise Financial.

I met one of my closest and dearest friends through the R.E.A.L. program. As an adult student immersed in a college culture centered mainly on the minds of brilliant, talented young individuals, the full-time program would otherwise have been isolating. To have someone to share those adult challenges such as home life and other responsibilities creates a bond like no other.

I still remember my graduation day in May of 1999. Two of my R.E.A.L. program classmates received their diplomas and waited at the end of the stage for my name to be called. As we walked back to our seats, arms linked together, I realized that I finally had time to ponder all that I had accomplished.

Marilyn Glazer-Weiser

Thanks to Professor Idelmanso and his Spanish Intermediate Composition and Conversation class at Tufts in the fall of 1999, I finally found my own voice. The topic of the writing and presentation assignment was an educational theme and he instructed us to get up in front of our classmates and talk about education en español without the benefit of notes.

From the first week of class I got the sense that he appreciated my work, participation, and passion for learning because he thanked me, his only non-traditional student, for being his student. It can be argued that my opportunity to study at Tufts in my mid-forties was probably even more precious to me than the opportunity presented to all of my classmates because they were all the same age as my children.

This was going to be my chance to allow my classmates to feel more comfortable with me as one of them. As my classmates raised their hands and asked me questions about my choice of timing to attend university and my plans for the future, I spoke more and more to them in a voice that was emerging for the most part, for the first time in my life. This voice was not just the voice of the words and phrases of my third language, Spanish, but it was the voice that had been trapped inside of me for such a long time because I had learned to hold myself back for the benefit of others, members of my family, my former spouse, members of my community, former teachers and bosses.

When I was in sixth grade, the talk at the end of the year was about which junior high school our teacher would recommend for each of her pupils. My English teacher, Miss Cronin, was the strictest teacher in the building. She used to be an attorney before she made her career switch to education. Since the City of Boston is so large, there were a few choices of appropriate schools in the district. When she said that I should be in the group of students attending Girls' Latin School in the coming fall, I gulped because I knew that I could not even think of going to Latin School. My two step-brothers were not as scholastic as I was and because I was a girl who was accustomed to being verbally and physically beaten every day by my step-mother and her two sons, I chose to not even let them know Miss Cronin thought that I was smart enough to attend Girls' Latin School—a prestigious exam school. So in the spring of 1963 I locked this precious memory into my heart and there it stayed until the summer of 1999.

My academic advisor at North Shore Community College also graduated from Tufts University's R.E.A.L. program, after completing her first two years of college at NSCC, as I did. We had coffee a few weeks before orientation at Tufts. She demanded to know if I knew what I was getting in for by attending Tufts University. She said that all of my classmates at Tufts were "A" students just like me. When I smiled so broadly that she could not ignore my happiness she wanted to know what I thought was so funny. My response was, "Oh, Marcey, I am finally going to Girls' Latin School!"

I am now a teacher myself, having graduated from the Applied Linguistics Program at the University of Massachusetts and I hope to inspire others as I have been inspired.

Legacy

Many R.E.A.L. students are the first in their family to attend college. Their success creates a pattern of achievement that has led many of their family members to further their education themselves, some of whom have attended Tufts.

Tina Johnson

Q: Could you please tell me why you decided to go back to college?

A: I was working full time in a parks and recreation department in northern Virginia. I developed community-based programs. I helped promote the preschool and the after-school programs. I even designed programs for senior citizens and other things that the community needed. The problem was that I could not make the lateral move to another county which paid better and had programs that I was more interested in because I did not have the needed bachelor's degree. So, I was stuck. I think I was 23 at the time and it felt like I was too young to be stuck. So I took advantage of the tuition assistance at the government positions that would pay for two classes a year at a community college.

It was the first time in my life that I had a love of learning. I had a couple of great professors who took an interest in me. After my first developmental psychology class I decided that I was going on to get my bachelor's in this field and I would become a professor after that. I was going to get my Ph.D. and change my vocation completely.

Q: What was your high school like?

A: I wasn't really involved in high school. I had a lot of responsibilities at home. I had three younger brothers and some family issues. I was responsible for taking care of my brothers and did not have a lot of time for engaging myself in what could have been there. I was on the general track, which was

118   Diversity, Resiliency, Legacy

not the college bound track. Looking back now, I realize that the students who were the less affluent students were the ones who were put on the general track in my high school.

Q: How long did you spend at the community college?

A: I think it was two or three years part-time taking only one or two classes a semester. The drive to the college was an hour each way from where I was living. I also had to go after work.

Q: How did you learn about Tufts? Why did you decide to transfer to Boston?

A: I actually had a professor at the community college who wanted me to go to Harvard where she went. She had a colleague there in whose research I was very interested. I even met him and talked to him. And although I wasn't sure that Harvard would be the right environment, I was looking. I had never had anybody tell me that I could go to a school like that. I also applied to Tufts. When I called, they were so nice that I decided very quickly that Tufts was a better match for me than Harvard. Especially in the application process, Harvard made it very difficult for non-traditional students to apply. Very difficult. They also required me to report my parents' income, which I don't feel is even appropriate for me as an adult. They were not going to pay for me to go to school. It was very, very difficult. And at Tufts, when I called and spoke to someone in the admissions office, they said: "Oh, you want to apply to the R.E.A.L. program."

Q: Did you have family support while you were applying?

A: I was pretty much on my own. My father was not happy about me leaving. I hadn't lived with him since I graduated from high school. But I only lived ten minutes away from him all those years. I was independent. I also had one of my brothers living with me and I had to tell him that I was leaving. He was 21 at that time. Old enough to leave the nest but it was difficult for him. But I had to do it.

Q: How was your first semester at Tufts? How was the transition for you?

A: Hard. It was exciting. I enjoyed the other R.E.A.L. students very much. I quickly became involved in the R.E.A.L. Student Organization and was the activity coordinator one year. I was grateful. When I got to meet other

R.E.A.L. students, I felt really welcome and also felt that when I started classes that I enjoyed the other undergraduate students. I know this is not always the case but they were like younger siblings to me. I was twenty-five so it was very comfortable for me from the beginning. The first semester I spent a great deal of time in the math department with Math 4, which is the requirement for most R.E.A.L. students. I spent more time in the math department than any other place on the campus. I had a lot of other R.E.A.L. students to study with. I also found out that the psychology department was not a great match for me, even though I ended up getting my bachelor's in psychology. But the child development department was a better fit for me even though I don't study children but creativity.

Professor David Henry Feldman in child development was a better match for me as far as my research interests were concerned. But I finished my bachelor's in the psychology department and now I am finishing my master's in the child development department. And I have been accepted into the Ph.D. program, so I will be a triple Jumbo.

Q: Were you involved in any research while an undergraduate or graduate student at Tufts?

A: Oh, yes. I am doing a case study now on the poet Deborah Digges. I am looking at the relationship between her intellectual development, her field of expertise, and her personal life, in particular the obstacles she had to overcome and how they relate to the development of her expertise.

Q: How would you describe your undergraduate life?

A: Well, I think it was somewhat different from the experience of the traditional-age students. The difference is in the perspective. I knew very clearly why I was here. It wasn't really to discover myself, although I have changed a lot while being here. But I came very businesslike knowing what I wanted to do, what I wanted to study and what I wanted to accomplish. Some undergrads have very clear goals, and some of them are very young and they don't know yet. I had to work throughout my undergraduate career and that was a constraint on my time. I think socially it was very different. Most of my socializing was with other R.E.A.L. students but I had a few friends who were undergraduates in the commuter house with whom I am still friends today. They were only a couple of years younger than me.

120   Diversity, Resiliency, Legacy

Q: I want to go forward and ask you about your last semester at Tufts. Did you already know that you were accepted to the master's program here?

A: I was accepted to Tufts' master's program during my last semester. I didn't want to leave Tufts. I looked at other programs and because of David Henry Feldman's work and mine being so closely related and there being only two other people in the country who do what he does, I was very limited where it would be appropriate for me to go. Again, I applied to Harvard to study with Howard Gardner but he is getting older and I don't even know if he is taking graduate students. So, for me it was really a matter of only having very few places in the country that were appropriate to my area of interest. It was an easy decision to stay here. Plus you get offered a substantial financial break to stay. I can continue my research uninterrupted by staying. And I think that Tufts is a place that does try to cultivate their own. It seemed like a good place to begin. And end.

Q: You will be beginning your Ph.D. studies next year. What are your plans afterwards?

A: I think I should teach some other places, to understand how things can be different at other universities, for the perspective.

Q: What do you think is your biggest gain from being a R.E.A.L. student?

A: Independence. Out of all the members of my family, I will be able to buy a home as a woman without having a husband. Knowing that I can provide for myself, knowing that I can do the work, contribute to the body of literature that I rely on and that way change the world like we all do in our own way. When I was limited in my job before, it was because I did not have the background that I needed. Now I have a kind of security that I have never had and never knew that I could have. If you would have told me when I was in high school that I could go to college, I would not have believed it. Especially one like Tufts. I mean, I may choose to get married one day but I know that now I can do it on my own. I actually left Virginia practically engaged. Now if I choose to be in that position again, it will be in a different way.

Q: How is that different from the Tina who was graduating high school?

A: Well, I graduated from high school with a degree in cosmetology and not with many tools to work well in the real world, without much independence. It was kind of a minimal way to live. I lived a very simple life, which is

Jean Herbert and Tina Marie Johnson 121

something to which I aspire again, but in a different way. There were many times when if my car broke down, I would be desperate. I often lived in poverty, growing up as a child and then as a young woman, and still now as a graduate student and I will be for a long time paying off my loans, but that is not really the point. It's the fact that I will be able to provide for myself; I will be able to do work that in my mind contributes to the world around me.

Q: If you would meet a prospective R.E.A.L. student who is about to apply to Tufts, what would your message be?

A: The R.E.A.L. students come from such various backgrounds. I think I would tell the person to go to a community college first and have some success there. And then if they love it, they should apply regardless if they can figure out how they are going to do it, how it will work. Because if you think in advance how are you going to pay the rent, take your children to school, and how are you going to survive, you can drive yourself crazy and then not apply. My advice would be just to do it. If you love the work and you want the opportunity in life, just apply. And don't think about the details, it will all fall together.

Soledad Montanes-Ordovas

Q: Would you tell me about your life prior to your decision to enroll at Tufts University?

A: I came to the United States from Barcelona in 1982 because my husband got a doctoral scholarship and we were planning to be here for one year. But one year led to another and another and we have been here for 23 years now. I was only able to go to college for two years back in Spain, and I had always wanted to finish. I had to work for family reasons. I worked for a number of years, but I always wanted to go back to college, and in Spain, they don't have a program for students 25 and older. I did not speak English when we first came. Back in Spain in high school, I had studied French, not English.

I started taking ESL (English as a Second Language) classes. I was working at the time as a receptionist, and after that, I was only taking courses pretty much part time, until 1988. We were expecting our first child and I decided to go to school full time because I wanted to take as many courses as possible before our child was born. I graduated from Tufts when he was one year old. Then I applied for my master's at Tufts, in Child Study. I received my master's degree in 1992.

I don't know if you still have the weekly meetings for the first semester students, but I found them to be really helpful and very well tuned because we shared our problems. Every now and then some of your co-students would give you suggestions such as how to work out problems. Wow. It was tough, I have to tell you, it wasn't easy, because I had a family and I was working and it was difficult. So, at the end, when my son was born and I had to do

123

124   Diversity, Resiliency, Legacy

the homework and the reading after I put him to bed at night, sometimes I didn't know I could make it. But we all kind of helped each other, as I am sure you do now; that is how we managed. And I always felt that every paper I turned in, every exam I took, I was a step closer.

Q: What did you major in?

A: As an undergraduate I majored in child study and I also took some courses in Spanish literature.

Q: So, you came here to a new country and your plan was to stay a limited time and probably to go back, if I understood well. Am I correct?

A: At the beginning, yes. My husband thought that the scholarship would last for a year at most and then we would go back, but we both like it here and at the time he was offered a job so we decided to stay.

Q: How would you say your experience at Tufts differed from that of the regular undergraduate?

A: I think it was really different because on the one hand, I was not living on the campus. We lived in Newton. We were renting a very small apartment. We quickly realized when we had our first child that we had to move. We needed a little bit more space so he could crawl around and walk around. So, then we started to look for a house and moved to Framingham. We have been here for fifteen years.

But we did things with the R.E.A.L. program, not just the meetings, but social events like a BBQ. I tried to stay involved with that. I must say, I never felt bad about being an older student, I always felt ok and accepted. When I had my first child, I would bring him with me to school and when I had class   some students babysat my child while I was in class. Sometimes they took him to the dorms, or apartments, and sometimes they took him to the campus center, and when the weather was nice in the spring they would walk around the campus with the stroller. I remember that the R.E.A.L. students had a little house where we met, near the campus center. I went there sometimes between classes.

Q: What was your relationship with your professors? How did they see you?

A: I think we had good relationships. The reason I continued to go ahead and apply for my master's was because one of the courses that I had to take to fulfill a requirement was Intro to Child Study. The professor who taught the course was Dr. Camara and for me she was the person who really sparked my interest in this field. Every now and then you meet a professor and you go "wow". She was a WOW professor. She was amazing. Her lectures, her classes were really interesting. So when I completed my undergraduate studies, I really wanted to go ahead and do my master's in child study and I was lucky enough to take another couple of classes with her as a graduate student. She was my advisor for child study.

Q: Where did you go after graduate school?

A: I finished my master's, and graduated in May of 1992. I was expecting my second child. She was born in October and I stayed at home until she was in second grade. And then I went back to work. One of the jobs I had before I went to Tufts was babysitting. One case in particular influenced me. He was seven days old when I started. And for about a year and a half I took care of him and the day he started to walk, his parents were at work. And then I said to myself that it is not good to miss that. Experiencing that told me that if I ever had a child, I wanted to be at home when this happens. And because of the job my husband does, he travels a lot, I felt that one of us had to stay at home. Now I work at an elementary school; we have kindergarten through 5th grade. We have almost 500 children. I work mostly with the families in a program. It gives me satisfaction when I can help someone who just came to the country and cannot speak the language.

Q: What does your husband do?

A: He is a professor at Tufts, in the graduate school of nutrition on the Boston campus. He received his degree the same year I got my bachelor's degree. But what happened at the commencement ceremony was that he had to be with the graduate students. And I did not have anyone who could keep an eye on my baby. So, I put him into my baby carrier on my back. And I made him a cap and gown. He was one year old and refused to wear the cap. He was not walking yet. And as we were lining up someone took a picture of my baby and me. I had him in the backpack with both of us in cap and gown. And the following year, in 1990, they used it for the back cover of the brochure they give out at the commencement. And now he is a senior in high school and has been accepted at Tufts. The boy who was born in 1988 will enter Tufts in the fall of 2007. I was trying to find that picture to show him before you called. We are really happy that he is going to Tufts.

Delores Huff

I have written about my experiences as a chapter in a book entitled <u>Teaching From a Multi-cultural</u> <u>Perspective,</u> Helen Roberts, Editor, Sage Publications. My chapter was entitled "On Becoming a Mensch or a Mentor." It describes my first year at Tufts.

I was one of the first ten adult students Tufts accepted in a grand experiment in 1969. We were all poor. I was on welfare. We all had children. And we were all organizers. I was the organizer for the Boston Indian Council. There were eight black women organizers and one white welfare mother organizer.

I was interviewed by Beatrice Miller (she later became a Dean or President of a college in Chicago) and by the President of Tufts. I never took the SAT. They said it wasn't relevant anyway at my age. I was the youngest of our group at age 35. We called ourselves "The Over-the-Hill Gang."

I have many stories to tell, but this will suffice for now. Tufts knew it had a strange new undergraduate population with untested academic skills. But it also knew that we had a track record of success and that meant we were bright and took on challenges. Tufts also knew that in a sea of 18 year olds well prepared for college, we would feel extremely insecure in spite of our successes. So it determined that whatever it could do, it would, to make this experiment a success. And it did.

It set up a special study room for us. Judy Laskaris ran a special seminar for us. We learned to write academically. There were loads of other strategies they used, not the least of which was that we could talk to the Dean whenever

128   Diversity, Resiliency, Legacy

we felt insecure. And they made sure that we had sufficient money for books and transportation, and the feds took care of our tuition.

How well did we do? After Mary Goode graduated she won a seat in the state legislature. Another ran a health center in Roxbury. One built and ran a school. I lost track of so many of them. I developed the Boston Indian Center, and took my doctorate at Harvard. I later ran an Indian School in South Dakota and became a professor at California State University, Fresno. I am now Professor Emeritus of American Indian Studies.

Richard May

Q: What is your family's educational background?

A: I'm the first person in my family to go to college, and the first on my mother's side to graduate from high school.

Q: Could you describe a typical day in your life prior to deciding to attend college?

A: I was working as a vocational instructor for adults with mental and/or physical disabilities. My responsibilities included job procurement and integration in the workplace, teaching occupational and social skills, and acting as a liaison between my clients and the community to ensure their rights were protected. I was in that position for ten years. Prior to that job, I was a Deadhead. I spent close to seven years following the Grateful Dead around the US. I sold tie-dyed wall-hangings and vegetarian food to support myself.

Q: Did you do this right after high school?

A: When I graduated high school, my parents didn't support my desire to study art, so I rebelled. I left home to follow the Grateful Dead. For me, it was an opportunity to discover a lot about myself and about how the world works. I used to joke that I didn't get a formal education, but my "Deaducation" was a good replacement.

Q: Why did you choose to go to college?

130 Diversity, Resiliency, Legacy

A: Honestly, I got tired of having friends and colleagues tell me I was too smart to have not gone to college. I mean…I knew I was intelligent, but it just didn't happen for me the way it did for others. Also, because I worked for the state of Connecticut, a management level position required at least a bachelor's degree. Without it, there was no way for me to advance in my job. I started going to school two nights a week to earn my associate's degree.

Q: How did you learn about Tufts? Why the R.E.A.L. program?

A: The truth is that I was leaving a friend's house in Somerville after a weekend visit. I got lost trying to get back on the Mass Turnpike and ended up on the Tufts campus. I confess that I had not considered Tufts, but later that week I did some research. I found the Art History department to be small and it was staffed by leading scholars in the field. I decided it was wise to look more into what the university offered. I discovered the R.E.A.L. program. Talk about serendipity!

Q: How was your experience at Tufts?

A: What can I say? I LOVED attending Tufts. The faculty was outstanding and incredibly supportive of my education. The students were brilliant and came from all over the world (they even thought the older guy – me- was cool!). The academic environment was clearly geared at promoting individual success. It is a most excellent school all around. I am very proud to be an alumnus. I will stress that, if not for the R.E.A.L. program, I sincerely believe this entire experience would never have happened.

Q: You talk about individual success and its importance, how did you experience it at Tufts?

A: My academic record at Tufts was very important to me. I know GPAs aren't everything, but they certainly help you assess your performance and reinforce the hard work you put into your studies. Because succeeding in whatever I do is important to me, it was necessary that I do well at Tufts. I am very proud of graduating summa cum laude and for receiving the History of Art Prize for 1999. I worked hard to achieve both and it was extremely gratifying.

Q: Did you join clubs, organizations?

A: When I first arrived on campus, I got involved with the gay, lesbian, and trans-gendered group. I really felt that I could offer support to young gay people who might be struggling with their sexual orientation. Unfortunately,

Jean Herbert and Tina Marie Johnson   131

I soon realized that as an adult learner, I didn't have the time or schedule to allow for me to participate regularly.

Q: What was your major? And why?

A: I studied Art History. I had traveled extensively throughout Europe and visited many art museums, cathedrals and historically significant architectural sites. I loved it! My mind seemed to soak up everything I learned and experienced and I started to independently study and research western art. Interestingly, I was always a horrible history student (I passed US History in high school with a 60 average!). Studying Art History opened the door to understanding the world's past and how people living at the time viewed their world. It certainly gives one insight into the world you are living in, too.

Q: Were you involved in some research, work-study, or other similar programs during your studies?

A: During my senior year, I had an internship at an historic home in Waltham. H.H. Richardson designed 'Stonehurst' and Frederick Law Olmsted designed the lawn. The original owner of the house was the grandson of a signer of the Declaration of Independence. Talk about a dream internship! I worked with the curator to accession the home's furnishings: art, antiques, decorative crafts and personal belongings.

Q: What are you doing now?

A: Currently, I own and operate a bed & breakfast in Louisville, Kentucky. It is an historic mansion built circa 1904. It is located in Old Louisville, the nation's third largest preservation district and within the largest contiguous neighborhood of Victorian mansions in the US. There are lots of ties here to Boston. Many of the homes in my neighborhood were modeled after H. H. Richardson's style, called Richardsonian Romanesque, and Olmsted designed the park system here. What odd coincidences!! Before finding the bed & breakfast for sale, I had no idea the neighborhood existed. "Finding" Old Louisville offered me a chance to use my education and background to become involved in historic preservation and cultural heritage tourism.

Honestly, it is quite exciting to end up somewhere you never dreamed of being and to come to the realization that all the steps you have taken in your life brought you there. It reminds me of something Joseph Campbell said:

132   Diversity, Resiliency, Legacy

"...if you do follow your bliss you put yourself on a kind of track that has been there all the while, waiting for you, and the life that you ought to be living is the one you are living. When you can see that, you begin to meet people who are in your field of bliss, and they open doors to you."

There is no doubt that the faculty and students I interacted with at Tufts, especially the R.E.A.L. program, were in my field of bliss.

Q: How was your relationship with the professors?

A: I really respected all of my professors at Tufts. My relationship with them was somewhat unique. I found that being a thirty-something guy with a beard and receding hairline made me stand out a bit. It certainly opened the door for communication! The professors always wanted to know 'my story' and what brought me to their classroom. Since I was close in age to some of my professors, I felt I could relate to them better.

Q: How was your relationship with other R.E.A.L. students? How did the R.E.A.L. program help you to go back to college, and actually how did it help you all the way to graduation?

A: I know it seems to be a cliché, but we really were like family. We shared our hardships and our successes. We laughed, we cried and we partied! In a situation such as an adult going to a top university to earn a degree, a support system is absolutely necessary. As I have previously mentioned, having peers who could relate to your particular situation really helped. Graduation was made particularly rewarding by the fact that those of us R.E.A.L. students who were receiving our degrees all sat together and walked together. Graduation was a very happy day for me.

Simply put, without the R.E.A.L. program, I would never have experienced the quality education I received at Tufts University. Dean Jean Herbert was passionate about the adult learners program and did everything she could to get us whatever type of support we needed. As I said earlier, it is great to be around young people who respect you, but it was my peers who supported me. My circumstances were quite different from the younger students and they simply could not relate to them. I made very good friends through the bonding that naturally occurs in a program like R.E.A.L.. We were always there for one another...and I am sure we always will be.

Luis Martinez

About fifteen years ago, I came to this country as an immigrant from one of the poorest villages in rural El Salvador. I was seventeen years old. I later learned that most adolescents in the United States are getting ready for their high school prom at this age; instead, I had just completed a five thousand mile journey that took me from the dirt and mud covered roads of my native village in El Salvador to the streets of one of the most developed cities in the entire world. I left my country not because I didn't want to live there any more, nor because I decided that I did not want to be with my loving family any more. I left my country because there, young people like me did not have and still do not have opportunities to realize their dreams.

As any child I had many dreams. Even between the despair of poverty and the horrors of a civil war I found time for my favorite dreams; I had dreams to become a pilot so I could take an airplane high into the skies and be able to see the stars. I also dreamed of becoming the captain of a big ship so I could sail to distant places. For someone who had never seen the ocean, a ship or an airplane these were magical dreams. However, in my young fantastic mind I also had more realistic dreams. I dreamed about getting an education that could allow me to learn about the world, about life, about others but most important an education that could allow me to change my life. After thirty years, and after many struggles, many prayers and after many tears that dream has finally come true.

From the first day I set foot on the Tufts University campus I knew my life had changed forever. I had dreamed about that day for so many years and at last the R.E.A.L. program and Tufts University had allowed me to initiate my college education. I came with hopes and expectations. I also came with fright because I knew I was coming not only with my expectations but also with the expectations of so many people who in one way or another had believed in me and supported me throughout my journey. For the last four years I have carried out the dreams of my family, and the dreams and hopes of an entire immigrant Salvadoran community who see in me a dim but hopeful beam of light that would encourage many others to take and embrace the value of a great education.

Please forgive me if I have not been making too much sense, but what I want to say is that my education at Tufts University has enriched and changed my life forever and I want others to have the same opportunity that I had. I'm so grateful to the R.E.A.L. program for providing me with the opportunity to obtain my college education and for the unconditional support that I received and continue to receive from the university.

My learning experiences have transcended the walls of classrooms, lecture halls, and examination sessions. In the winter of 2004 I had the opportunity to visit Cuba along with 20 other Tufts students. The summer of that same year I went to El Salvador with a faculty member from The Fletcher School of Law and Diplomacy who was conducting a study on the Social, Psychological and Economical effects in the families of Salvadoran immigrants.

Without the opportunity that the R.E.A.L. program provided me, it's possible that getting an education would still be just a dream. However, today it's a bright and endearing reality that has forever changed not only my life but also the lives of many others in my family, my community, and my fellow immigrants in the Boston area. There are no words in my limited English vocabulary to explain with justice and with enough gratitude what the R.E.A.L. program means to me. It has allowed me to become the pilot of that airplane that as a little boy I dreamed would take me to see the stars; I have become the captain of that big ship that as a little boy I dreamed I would sail into the unknown seas. With all my heart, Muchas Gracias.

Erika Sonder

I started school in Germany during the war. I was 7 years old. I had 6 years of elementary school. During the war, schooling was haphazard. Schools were bombed out, and classes were often given in hotels or other public places. Sometimes there was no school for weeks as people moved from one place to another to escape the air raids.

After elementary school, we had to pass an exam to enter gymnasium (high school). I barely squeezed by, mostly by impressing everybody with my drawings. I attended for four years and then went to a commercial school in Lubeck to become a secretary. My family was torn apart by the war and we were very poor. So I decided to apply for an immigration visa at the U.S. Embassy in Hamburg. I wanted desperately to leave Germany.

I was interested in biology, and hoped to pursue my interest abroad. However, I met my husband right away in the U.S. and got married 7 months after arrival. I married at age 20 in the US and raised five children. At age 45 I realized that I wanted to become better educated. My children were growing up, two had finished college, a third was about to, and all that was left at home were my two daughters. An Austrian girlfriend of mine persuaded me to join her to get the GED, in order to go to college. She chickened out in the last minute, but I went and attended the classes and passed with flying colors.

Spurred on by that success, I applied to North Shore Community College as a part-time student. I stayed there for five years taking over 22 different courses, mostly science and English. After I received my associate's degree with a 4 point average, my teachers persuaded me to apply to a four-year college. I applied to Brandeis and Tufts and was accepted by both. I decided on Tufts, since it was a little closer to Manchester-by-the-Sea, where I lived until my divorce in 2000.

136   Diversity, Resiliency, Legacy

My daughter Claudia joined me at Tufts after one year. On the first day of classes I met Dr. Norton Nickerson, who persuaded me to take a double major in Environmental Studies and Biology. I enjoyed all my classes, although I had considerable trouble with Genetics. Claudia had to help a few of us with that difficult subject. After two tries I succeeded in getting a "C". Otherwise I managed mostly A's and B's. The only thing I joined was twice a trip with Dr.Nickerson's environmental class to the Bahamas. We called him Dr. Nick. He and his wife became good friends of mine after graduation. Unfortunately he died a few years ago, way too early!

Claudia and I both graduated in 1990 from Tufts, both with a B.S., she with honors. She was accepted to all the major veterinarian schools in the country, but decided to take residency in California for a year to qualify going to U.C.Davis for her Large Animal Vet. Degree as a citizen of CA. She worked her way through graduate school, which was a relief for us, having paid for five kids through college.

I waited for five years to continue my education to get an M.S. at Antioch New England Graduate School, which I received in 1998. In the time between graduating from Tufts and starting at Antioch I was a member of the Manchester-by-the-Sea Conservation Commission, and worked hard at preserving open space. I became a Vernal Pool expert, and by certifying a number of strategic vernal pools prevented a number of developments from taking shape in Manchester and Beverly.

After I graduated from Antioch I started my "Portable Herbarium" business. My botanical prints caught the attention of Dr. David Boufford at the Harvard University Herbarium, after he saw an article in the Sunday Boston Globe in early January 1999, which featured my prints on the front page of the North Shore Edition. A fellow Harvard professor had brought it to his attention. They asked me to come in to show my prints, and there I met Ray Angelo. He is the Curator of Vascular Plants for the New England Botanical Club at Harvard University. Dr. Norton Nickerson, a prominent member of the Club, had often talked to his environmental class at Tufts, to get in touch with Ray Angelo, in case they had botanical questions. I had never met Ray before, but to make a long story short, he and I really hit it off! He is my partner in life now! We live together here in Ipswich, in a house we built, and commute into Cambridge to attend to the N.E.B.C. collection of plants at the Harvard University Herbaria, mostly on weekends.

William

Q: Could you please tell me a little about your background?

A: I am from the southern part of Albania, but I was raised in Greece. Basically I spent my teenage years in Greece but I was going back and forth. Other than that I was just a regular student. Not really aiming at doing great in school; I was just playing sports. I was in an Albanian school until I was about ten and then Greek schools until 18.

Q: What did you do after high school?

A: Actually, when I was still in high school, I was trying to make it into the media world. I was trying many jobs. I was a model in magazines. I thought that I was becoming an actor. I wasn't even thinking about educating myself further. I was just thinking that the media world or being famous was a way I could make a good living and fulfill my dreams. But life is not all that. Life brings you things that you would have never imagined. So, after high school when I was about 19 or 20, I was diagnosed with a neurological problem. It was kind of hard for me to keep doing what I was doing. I started to have trouble getting around. When I was about 21, I came to the United States because the doctors in Greece were not really sure what was the problem. So, I came to the States to find out. I started to go to hospitals here right after my arrival. But I could not understand a word of English. I wanted to learn English.

Q: Did you come by yourself? That must have been difficult.

138   Diversity, Resiliency, Legacy

A: I came with my mother. We came straight to Boston. I came to the New England Medical Center. Actually, I remember that it was just one day before my birthday. It was November 20th, 1999.

Q: What made you determine that you might have a neurological problem?

A: It started as a weakness in my arms and legs. I had trouble walking. I stopped running. I stopped playing sports. I had trouble going up and down stairs. I had difficulty walking long distances. My doctor said that I should stay in the U.S. for a year. He was going to run some tests for a year. So I was having these treatments and at the same time he was trying to see if I am getting better. That was the program for a year.

Q: Did your mother stay as well?

A: She stayed for four months and then my father came for two months. After that I was on my own. I started to learn English and understand a little bit. It was easier to understand the language but harder to talk. I had trouble talking. And since my doctor said that this was nothing that would go away really fast, I said that I should forget about what I wanted to do before and I should try to really learn something and use it. I was thinking about studying graphic design or computers or web design. I went to Bunker Hill Community College in 2001 and started with ESL classes. Later I started to take some regular classes. I started doing really well in math. I would even tutor math later on. I thought that I was doing better than people who were born here or raised here. I don't want to sound egocentric but it gave me confidence. So I started to think about going to a different school. I had dreams about going to a better school.

Q: How did you learn about the R.E.A.L. program?

A: This is actually funny. They have a person at Bunker Hill that helps students to transfer to four-year colleges. The person there told me about the R.E.A.L. program at Tufts but I didn't pay attention. So later I started to take some classes at Harvard Extension School. You know, it is mainly a night school with little in common with Harvard. And then one night I was getting ready to sleep, and you know how you think before falling asleep about things, I thought I am taking classes at Harvard Extension but it is not really Harvard, what is the deal about that Tufts thing. So, I got up and went to my desk and logged on to the computer and checked. I found the website, I read about the R.E.A.L. program. I decided I was going to call the next day.

Q: So, you found out that it really is Tufts.

A: Yes. I applied in March 2004. When I got my acceptance letter, I cried a little bit. It was really exciting to get the letter.

Q: What were your first few weeks at Tufts like?

A: Well, the first semester was huge. I made it to Tufts. Then I went through some problems with my health. I started doing just ok. Now, I'm back on track. I mean I am thinking about graduating and going to graduate school after this.

Q: Did you have to overcome some other challenges?

A: Well, I am older than most of the other students. But that wasn't the problem. For me, it was difficult because the other students, well, at least the majority, came from private schools and were somewhat privileged. And, I am not poor but just average. There was a real difference there.

Q: How did you find the classes?

A: I found them more challenging than those at the community college. I decided that I wasn't dreaming about math so I changed my major to clinical psychology. I decided that I was lucky to be at Tufts because I have very good professors in terms of understanding their students and being there for them, and being passionate about their profession. Almost all of the professors at Tufts are so passionate about their subjects. They try to make you like what they like and I love that.

Q: What are your goals after Tufts?

A: I want to go to graduate school. Maybe Tufts' clinical psychology department. We'll see. I want to do something in psychology.

Q: Is there anything else you would like to add about the R.E.A.L. program?

A: I think it is amazing that you have this second chance after whatever you do. The R.E.A.L. program at Tufts gives you the opportunity to do what you were supposed to do. To study and educate yourself, do something good, better the future – your future and the future of the people around you. So, I think it is great to have a second chance.

Charles Paulding

Q: Charles, could you please describe a typical day in your life prior to coming back to college?

A: I was mostly doing menial work. You know, the kind of job that nobody is really interested in. I worked in warehouses and other places. None of it was really meaningful to me. I was about 25 when I decided to go back to school.

Q: Why did you choose to go back to school? What was your educational path?

A: I started at a community college in Massachusetts because I had done so poorly in high school. I was a terrible student in high school. I didn't study, I didn't take notes or show up to class. I just slept in class. So, consequently, I did not have a very good transcript after that. At the age of 25 I decided to change and went back to school. It had become really evident that what I was doing was not really working. I was not going anywhere. I had been reading a great deal in my free time. That helped me realize that I needed something more intellectually challenging in terms of work. And financially it was not working out well either. So, the two main reasons were the intellectual and the financial.

Q: What classes did you take?

142   Diversity, Resiliency, Legacy

A: I knew that my interest was in the sciences, but I was not sure if my major would be chemistry or biology. Originally, I thought I would be a chemist. And then I took chemistry at the community college with a really good professor who suggested that I should do some molecular biology since there are a lot of jobs in that field, and it is also an interesting field. So I started to take biology classes and more biology classes when I transferred from community college to U Mass Boston for a couple of semesters. I came to really enjoy it and was doing really well.

Q: How did you learn about Tufts?

A: It was part of my plan. I decided that I would go to a community college for a semester or two, and then to U Mass for a semester or two and then transfer to a better school, a more prestigious school in the area. I looked into Harvard, MIT, BU, and Tufts. I think that I learned about the R.E.A.L. program by flipping through the Tufts catalogue. And it seemed perfectly tailored to my needs as a returning student.

Q: Were you involved in other activities on the campus?

A: I was not involved in clubs; however, I started to do research after the first summer I was at Tufts. I got a job at the Tufts Medical School and continued on there for the remainder of my time at Tufts. I used to juggle my schedule so I had one day of the week free to go to the medical school and do research in molecular biology. I guess I was something of a nerd when I was in college. It was the complete opposite from how I was in high school. I worked really hard. My goals were to get As in everything.

Q: And did you?

A: Almost. French killed me. The only grades I got below an A were in French and Organic Chemistry.

Q: What role did the R.E.A.L. program play in your undergraduate life at Tufts?

A: It was nice to have the support, to talk to other people. You know, you get there and there is definitely a maturity difference, difference in interests and difference in background from the majority of the Tufts students. I came largely from a blue-collar background and most of the students at Tufts come straight from high school, have never really worked a crummy job.

Jean Herbert and Tina Marie Johnson 143

Q: You said that you graduated in 1995. What was your path after that?

A: I went immediately to graduate school, the Biological Environmental Sciences program at Harvard. I didn't take a break at all. You know, I did not really set out originally when I went back to school to get a PhD.. I know my original goal was to achieve academic excellence. I found myself a long way from the bottom of my class in high school, when I ended up at Harvard and Tufts. In that regard, it was an interesting journey. I came to realize that if I really wanted to be a scientist, I needed to have a Ph.D.. When I was at Tufts finishing my undergraduate work, I applied to ten graduate schools. Quite frankly, I was shocked when I got into pretty much all of them. While getting my doctorate, I worked at Mass General Hospital doing research, mostly cancer, cancer genetics and molecular biology. After I finished, I stayed on as a post-doc in the lab I was in but just while I was looking for a job. I ended up taking a job with Novartis that allowed me to continue to work on genetics.

Q: What is your job now?

A: I work as a genetic analyst mainly for pharmaceutical genetics. We do genetics studies on clinical trials and we are trying to correlate the variations of people's DNA to differences in responding to drugs or other aggressive events. We are trying to identify, genetically, subgroups of people, who are perhaps more prone to adverse events. Maybe we can develop a diagnostic test that would allow us to predict the outcomes. It is a very new field.

Q: How would you say your life is different now from before your time at Tufts?

A: It is completely different in many respects. It's funny, though. Even though my life is different, I'm not really that different. You know, I used to do lots of these menial jobs, and I was just as intelligent as I am now. Now I just have the kind of pedigree to do what I do. There are certain assumptions that go along with that. I guess the most important thing is my satisfaction with what I am doing, the direction my life is heading, that was the main reason I went back to school. Now, I am pretty happy. I am doing interesting work and have a decent living. I used to be really poor and there was a lot of frustration around not being able to use all of your intellect. I have always suspected that I was reasonably intelligent but you don't really know it until you test it.

Q: Did your family expect you to go to college?

144   Diversity, Resiliency, Legacy

A: No. A lot of these things are generational. My parents didn't go to school; my grandparents didn't go to college. The pattern kind of gets set and you are raised in that way. It was not the priority. That is generally how it is passed down. I kind of grew up in an upper middle class neighborhood. Even though my family was poor, a lot of my friends came from families with lots of doctors and lawyers and so forth. So, they were open to going to college from when they were three years old. I kind of tagged along with them to some extent. I got a glimpse of that. All of my friends went to college. And it was actually kind of funny because they took all the college bound classes and when I finally got to college, I did a lot better than many of them in college. I think they all got a kick out of it as well.

Q: Are you the first one to graduate from college in your family?

A: Yes. I have two siblings and both of them went on to school after I did. I have a lot of cousins who also took this path. It is interesting. I think that most of the R.E.A.L. students had similar experiences. My family got a big kick out of me going back to school.

Q: If you would meet a person who is thinking about going back to school, what would be your advice?

A: Definitely go for it. It was great. I loved going back to school. I wish I could keep doing it. I just thoroughly enjoyed Tufts. I had a great time. It is just such a pleasure to get to go to the classes every day. It has its moments when it wears on you, but to some extent that is life anyway. You have deadlines and work pressure situations so it is not that different. But I loved the environment. I guess that I would have enjoyed it even better if I had some money because I would not have had the enormous pressure to have to work. But it was certainly worthwhile. And it completely changed what I do for my life.

My wife and I are adopting a baby girl from China and I will be able to support a family now.

Gitta Rohweder

Q: What were you doing before you enrolled at Tufts?

A: I got out of high school in Germany in 1975 and came to the States, got married and had children. So, I was a mom. I was taking care of my small children. At first I was taking classes at NYU: calculus, chemistry and biology. Then I had a baby. I always had the plan of doing pre-med and going back to college. So, when I applied to Tufts, it was really a decision to go to college full time and go on with that plan.

Q: Why did you decide on Tufts?

A: At that time, we lived in New York and we were about to move to Boston. So, I applied to Tufts, BU, and also to Harvard. Tufts kind of appealed to me. They had the international curriculum, had an international community. The fact that there was a medical school attached to it was also attractive. I did not know about the R.E.A.L. program when I applied; I found out about it within the application process. It seemed like a good way to go to college and have other people around me who were in the similar state of mind, who weren't partying Saturday night.

Q: How old were your children at this point?

146   Diversity, Resiliency, Legacy

A: I think I started at Tufts in 1980, so my son was 2 and my daughter was 4. My son was just starting nursery school. It was difficult to make the transition from being able to do everything at home and taking care of family to delegating more and accepting help at home. It was only after my mother organized an au pair from Germany that I could really concentrate on school. But there was a transition period.

Q: How was your first year at Tufts?

A: It was really exciting. I was just really glad to be back in college. That is all I remember. A whole new world was opening up. I was finally back to learning something, you know. But I also got into some difficulties. For example, the fact that I had to study. I hadn't studied formally for years. It was painful. And also often I could not start studying until 8 or 8.30 because I was busy between 4 and 8.30 with the kids' homework, the dinner, and all that stuff. It was hard to find a study routine.

Q: How were your relationships with the professors as an older student?

A: I think that I had a good relationship with the professors. I liked my professors and I liked my classes. Also as an older student I was not afraid of raising my hand and saying something or even to be critical at times. But I don't think I went overboard with that.

Q: Were you involved in some other projects, clubs, going abroad programs at Tufts?

A: During my senior year, I did some biology research. I got to know the group of molecular biologists at Tufts pretty well. I didn't do anything else really. I could not. But I also went to the shows at the campus theater.

Q: Why did you decide to go to Tufts Medical School?

A: The decision to go to a medical school was pretty clear already in 1976. It just took me ten years to get there. And Tufts Medical School? Well, I was accepted as an early decision applicant. So, I only applied to Tufts Medical School. I got in and that was that.

Q: What is it that made you want to become a doctor?

Jean Herbert and Tina Marie Johnson   147

A: There are a lot of doctors in my family so that was one reason. It was familiar to me. I wanted to work with people. That was pretty clear to me. And my father was a hospital minister. When I was eighteen I thought that he had an important job helping the people, talking to them when they were sick or dying. Also, I was always interested in disease processes and all the omnipresent questions of how people get sick, how to live healthy. What I like now about medicine is that you work with people. You build a body of knowledge that can be viewed from different sides. It is a profession that gets better with time. You have to keep yourself up to date with fresh ideas, and new ways of doing things. I also worked in a nursing home to see if I am right for this job. At that point I made the decision that I wanted to do medicine. But it took me until 1986 to get into the medical school.

Q: What did you do after med school? Where did you go? You are in Norway now. But how did you get from Tufts Medical School to Norway?

A: I graduated the Tufts Medical program in 1990. And then I was a resident at St. Elizabeth in Brighton for three years. In 1994, I got a job as an internist at the South Shore Hospital. I worked there until 2001. And in 1999, when my children were already grown and in college and I was ready for another experience I took a job and moved to Norway.

Q: How do you enjoy being back in Europe?

A: Even though the culture is different, it does not seem foreign to me because I grew up in Germany. Coming from the States and being trained in the States, finding my place in the hospital was somewhat difficult. At this point I am fluent in the language and can function here to the fullest.

Q: Are you enjoying it then?

A: Yes. I am an internist at a stroke unit working with patients in the acute phase right after they come to the hospital and up to ten days. Then they get discharged to rehab or to home. It is a Scandinavian model of a stroke unit. It is a little different from what they have in the States. It is run by the Internal Medicine Department here in this town I am in and it is actually used as a model internationally for this kind of work. It is a very multidisciplinary environment and I enjoy that very much. It is a university hospital so we have medical students and residents and I am actually the head of the student

148   Diversity, Resiliency, Legacy

teaching of our unit. I am fifty per cent positioned at the hospital and fifty per cent at the university as a lecturer. We have about a hundred students a year and they all spend about a week in our unit. They learn about stroke and stroke patients.

Q: Would you do it again, I mean be a student at a later time, all over again?

A: Yes. I had done a lot of studying while I had children. The learning process became a part of the family and both of my kids have done really well and have gone on to be responsible citizens. So, also from the side of parenting, I think it had a positive effect even though when you ask them there were also some negatives. I was always busy.

Thomas Payne

Q: Could you describe a typical day in your life prior to deciding to return to college?

A: I graduated from high school in a relatively large city located in central North Carolina and decided to join the family heating and air conditioning business while the majority of my friends went off to college. About one year later, I began taking classes at a local college on a full-time basis. I took classes for a semester, and although I did well, I never felt as though I belonged there. I took another year off from school to earn more money and tried to return on a part-time basis, but never regained my academic focus. I had also become used to a style of living that required a full-time income. So, I dropped out after only one semester and returned to the family business.

About a year later, I moved to Hartford, CT when my fiancé graduated from college. There, I continued to work in the service industry for some time. Not happy with my situation, I worked as a waiter and bartender at restaurants with the intention of taking classes during the day. As you might imagine, this did not work out so well with the late nights and "party" mentality common to that line of work.

Q: Why did you choose to go to college again?

A: Soon after getting married, I came to the realization that I was not meeting my potential and just coasting through life. I decided to go back to school knowing that I would have to make a full-time commitment to keep my focus

150   Diversity, Resiliency, Legacy

on my studies. My wife and I moved to a less-expensive suburb of Hartford where I attended a local community college. I was fortunate enough to find a job at an optical lab with a very understanding owner who was willing to let me work around my academic schedule.

Q: Were your family, friends, and work colleagues supportive of your decision?

A: My wife and her family were very supportive of my decision to go back to school. She came from a family of well-educated engineers, scientists and teachers with degrees from such institutions as MIT, UNC and Duke. They had always seen my potential even when the vision eluded me. Without their support, I would have never taken the chance. Needless to say, I was terrified of failure and felt that I would not only disappoint myself, but my family and supporters as well. After only one semester, I realized that this was something that I not only needed to do but wanted to do. Once I received my grades from the first semester, I knew that only I had been holding myself back. I went on to obtain my associate's degree from Manchester Community and Technical College (MCTC) with nearly a 4.0 GPA.

Q: How did you learn about Tufts?

A: During my studies at MCTC, I rediscovered the world of mathematics and engineering. As I had always been fascinated by structures, architecture and how things work, I was confident that I wanted to pursue a career in engineering. After many discussions with the two professors at MCTC that I really connected with, I researched northeastern universities with the top rankings for Civil Engineering. I came to the decision to apply to UCONN, Tufts, RPI, WPI and Rutgers as a transfer student. Shortly after applying to Tufts, Marian Connor contacted me and invited me to transfer to Tufts as part of the R.E.A.L. program. She explained the concept of the R.E.A.L. program and I was intrigued. Since Tufts was my first choice, I gladly accepted her invitation.

Q: How was your experience at Tufts? Did you find the R.E.A.L. program helpful?

A: As an undergraduate student, I did feel quite out of place at Tufts. The atmosphere was much different than that of MCTC. The students were younger and less mature. Many of the students that I met seemed to only be there because they had to be, unable to appreciate the opportunity that had been afforded them. And since my wife was unable to get a transfer from Hartford, I really felt alone and out of place.

Fortunately, the support of the R.E.A.L. program was there to help me through this transition period. I made friends with other R.E.A.L. students who are still my friends today. Because we were all in an engineering program, we easily related and frequently met just to discuss our difficulties and brag about our successes. I was also able to connect with some of the graduate students who were teaching assistants and lab instructors for the courses that I was taking.

Eventually, I also met some younger students who took their studies as seriously as I did. We formed a study group and met frequently to work on various projects. Although I was placed into the role of the group leader or tutor, I felt that I gained a lot from the experience and it helped me stay focused on my work.

I went on to graduate summa cum laude in 1995, at the top of my class (yes #1) with a B.S. in Civil and Environmental Engineering. I continued my education at Tufts as a graduate student and obtained my M.S. in 1996. Although I was no longer officially associated with the program, I was told that I would always be part of the R.E.A.L. family.

Q: Did you join clubs, organizations? Were you involved in some research, work study, or other similar programs during your studies?

A: As an engineering student and a husband, time for extracurricular activities was limited, especially with my weekly commute to the Hartford area. I joined the Tufts student chapter of the American Society of Civil Engineers (ASCE) and acted as an officer in the organization. I also competed in the concrete canoe competition and the steel bridge competition, each for two years straight. The great thing about these competitions was that they were actually working projects where we got to design every aspect of our canoes and bridges and then build our design. These competitions were extraordinary learning adventures.

Q: What did you do after graduation?

A: I continued with my graduate studies immediately after obtaining my B.S.. However, I did take one year in a "Mr. Mom" role after obtaining my M.S.. Presently, I am a Senior Environmental Engineer with The Louis Berger

152   Diversity, Resiliency, Legacy

Group, Inc., where I have designed entire military bases for overseas locations, as well as small infrastructure improvements for local municipalities. I found that the maturity and determination that helped me achieve my goals as a student at Tufts have carried over into my career.

Q: How was your relationship with the professors?

A: As an older student, I found that it was much easier to relate to the professors and for them to relate to me. My relationships with my professors were, for the most part, ones of mutual understanding and respect.

Q: How was your relationship with regular undergraduate students?

A: I found that the majority of the students in the engineering program were remarkably focused and intent on excelling. For this reason, we were able to relate to one another and formed excellent working relationships and some social bonds. However, I also found some students, both in engineering and liberal arts, that had a "holier-than-thou" attitude. I had no use for these students.

Q: Are you the first person in your family to have a 4-year degree?

A: On my side of the family, I am the first to obtain a bachelor's degree.

Marcey Marold

Q. What were you doing before coming to Tufts?

A: I was with TWA for twenty-two years in various capacities and, at the time that I returned to school, we were in a major labor dispute. This went on for well over a year so it was during that period that I decided to go back to school. That's when I went to North Shore Community College. Eventually we were called back by the airline and I flew international for six months. But the environment was very negative and besides, I had been taking many courses by that time and I didn't want to stop going to school. So, I decided to resign.

Q: How did you hear about the Tufts R.E.A.L. program?

A: I was in the Honors Program at North Shore and the director there recommended it to me. I transferred to Tufts with Eileen Fisk, my best friend. We had known each other from the airline and North Shore. At Tufts, we didn't necessarily take the same classes, but we tried to schedule them so that we could commute back and forth together. And both of us, as I said, because of the airline strike, had a lot of part-time jobs and so, we were pretty busy. We took demanding classes and then, oftentimes, worked at night at a job to make ends meet. Consequently, we didn't really get that involved in activities at the university. But the R.E.A.L. program and getting to know the other students in the program really helped.

Q: What other support systems did you have?

154   Diversity, Resiliency, Legacy

A: My parents were very supportive. At the time they were living in Illinois. Then they came out and they were very, very supportive. They were very supportive of me going back to school but were a little bit concerned that I would resign from a job that I had for so long and I was at that point at the top of the pay scale so I had been making some pretty good money flying international. Of twenty-two years that I was with TWA, twenty of those years I was in management.   So my parents were being pragmatic about things, but they were very supportive of the fact that I wanted to go back to school. And my brother, too, actually. I think that I was probably the influence for him going back to school himself, eventually.

Q: So what happened after Tufts?

A: After Tufts I decided to go to grad school. There was a program at UMass/ Boston that attracted me because they were going to start a new doctorate program in Linguistics. Ultimately, the program didn't get approved, so I ended up getting my master's in English. But I really liked doing that.

Q: What are you doing now?

A: After I got my master's degree, I came back to North Shore and started teaching in the English department part-time. It was just a wonderful experience being back at North Shore. I taught part-time for about three years and my predecessor retired and so, the Honors Program position was open. I applied and I got it. To be able to coordinate the Honors Program after *being* an Honors Program student for a couple of years when I was here was just really a great experience. I used to think I would go back and get my doctorate and teach at a four-year college, but I have really found my true calling here. The students challenge me in so many ways. I'm very happy here. I have tenure now and I love teaching at a community college.

Friends of the R.E.A.L. Program

Bobbie Knable

Former director of the R.E.A.L. Program

In the sixties, when Americans saw education as a means to economic and social mobility, we discovered that access was limited for large segments of the population: some were too poor even for the public institutions, and entrance requirements to the most selective colleges excluded most of the those capable of doing the work but not conventionally prepared.

Encouragement to broaden educational opportunities to more students came from two major sources: the government, with educational grants and loans; and student demands for increased diversity. But it was the women's movement that awakened us to the need for increased opportunities for adult women.

A wealth of leadership talent had appeared when government subsidized various community self-help programs. Most of these women had never had a college course nor had even thought of themselves as having college potential when they were the age of traditional college students. They knew they were capable administrators and proved it by the jobs they held, but they also knew that they were not free to move outside those jobs unless they had more conventional--meaning college--credentials. Tufts recruited ten women, most of them urban minority women, and primarily those who held leadership positions in community organizations.

Antonia Chayes, Dean of Jackson, envisioned a comprehensive academic environment at Tufts that would include a day care center, a women's studies program, and educational opportunities for women from diverse racial and economic backgrounds to pursue a degree. At a time when most other programs denied institutional funds for financial aid to adult students, segregated them in "special" or "extension" degree programs, and

158   Diversity, Resiliency, Legacy

ignored the problems faced by adults in returning to or beginning a college education, Tufts provided financial aid, enrolled its adult students in the regular undergraduate program, and provided resources to help meet their academic needs, including a weekly seminar for credit and special college writing classes.

In 1976, the program was opened to men, many of whom had interrupted their study and, like the women, were returning to complete their degrees or had been encouraged by the community college experience to continue in a four-year program.

What began as the Continuing Education Program has evolved into the R.E.A.L. (Resumed Education for Adult Learners) Program, and it continues to attract and support women and men who might otherwise find access to a selective institution closed. The Day Care Center, established in 1971, is a flourishing part of the Tufts-Medford-Somerville communities, and the popularity of the Women's Studies Program grows stronger each year. The success of these programs is a tribute to the university's dedication to the original vision.

Written in 1990 for the 20th Anniversary of the R.E.A.L. Program

Marian Connor

Former director of the R.E.A.L. Program

Q: Mrs. Connor, could you please tell me about your involvement with the R.E.A.L. program?

A: I came to Tufts in 1977 and I had a split appointment between the English department and administration. I was a preceptor for commuting students. When they did away with the preceptor program, Dean Nancy Millburn asked me if I would like to take over the R.E.A.L. program. I was delighted. I had discussed some of the aspects of the R.E.A.L. program with Bobbie Knable, who was the director at that time, and it seemed like a wonderful program. It was still called Continuing Education then. It had begun as a program for women but had just begun admitting men. I think that was perhaps the first year. I liked every part of it. I liked the fact that I got to interview everyone who came in. We had a different application process from the traditional undergraduate admissions.

I also liked the fact that I was in close contact with the students through the weekly seminar and through their journals. It was a way not only of seeing what was going on with the individual students but also what people were obsessing about at any particular time. There is something special about people who will interrupt their lives at whatever point and come back to school. It is such a huge commitment.

I was the one who changed the name from Continuing Education to Resumed Education for Adult Learners because there were so many people who thought

160   Diversity, Resiliency, Legacy

CE meant taking some ditsy little course some place and that was it. But resumed education, I thought, said it more accurately. We actually painted the canon one night. When we changed the name of the program, some of the students I knew pretty well thought that we should do something to make everybody notice. So, we got up at some ungodly time in the morning, three o'clock or so, and we had orange paint because at that point the application folders for the R.E.A.L. students were orange and so we painted the canon orange. There were about six of us including my husband, who is an engineer from MIT. We had stencils and we put on the canon in perfect letters: "C.E. is R.E.A.L." It was against the rules back then but that was one of the sweet rules. The tradition to paint the canon started during the Vietnam War when people would go up to this canon and put flowers on it and paint peace symbols on it. Since it was against the rules, it was a big deal. And then some smart person said: "Let them paint the canon. Who cares?"

Q: What do you think are the difficulties that R.E.A.L. students have to overcome when they come to Tufts?

A: The finances are always difficult. Tufts is an expensive place. And it is also a huge time commitment. Some students might have an idea of how much it will change their lives, but most don't realize the time they will need to put into their work compared to their previous school.

Sometimes families and friends don't understand the demands made on the students. They have to learn to say no. For some it is also the transportation issue. They are all commuting students and they don't have it as easy as if they would be living in a dorm. They don't have that opportunity. That is another reason why I am a strong believer in the seminar because you want people to get to know each other and support each other. It is important for people to know that other people are experiencing some of the same difficulties. It is good to have a place, the lounge, where you can go and sit and have a cup of coffee.

Q: What do you think is the purpose of the R.E.A.L. program for Tufts but also for the community?

A: People can make a lot of wrong choices when they are 17 or 18. Life intervenes. Why should some really smart, wonderful person not be able to start all over again? They should have the chance to expand their world intellectually. I think it would be awful not to have that. And of course, many people don't have it, but Tufts has given this second chance to bright people who might have made a poor decision when they were young, or who might have had a difficult family situation or stopped their education for some reason.

Professors really appreciate the dedication that the R.E.A.L. students have. And I think that the R.E.A.L. students can be an example to the younger students who often have it a lot easier, especially if someone else is paying the bills. Not that I am against that, but I think if the younger students could appreciate a little bit more how hard the R.E.A.L. students work for their education, it might give them pause and they would appreciate how valuable their education is. But you know, the numbers are so small, it is hard to see how best to make an impact on the campus as a whole.

Q: Is there something you would like to add to this interview?

A: All I can say is that from my time at Tufts working with the R.E.A.L. students was absolutely, no question, the best part of my job. I taught English and I was senior class dean and did various things. I was pre-law advisor for a while but the best part was working with the R.E.A.L. students. I am just very grateful to have had that experience. Because I think it certainly has made me realize that not everybody has the same opportunities. You can really appreciate more what people do for an education. I didn't have to work that hard for my education and seeing how people will do it is really inspiring.

And after graduation they go on to do wonderful things. Everyone I know who has been in the program has benefited from it. And then they bring this benefit to their families and where they work. I don't know if these people are just gold to start with or if it is being a part of the program, but the people who went through the program are amazing people and they have gone on to do wonderful things and that benefits Tufts as well.

Frederick and Eleanor Pratt

Founders of the Pratt Scholarship in honor of Theresa Pratt

Q: Mr. and Mrs. Pratt, could you please tell me about your connection to the R.E.A.L. program? Especially, why did you choose to support it?

MRS. PRATT: We are doing this in memory of our daughter, Theresa, who died after her freshman year. She adored Tufts. She had the best year. Her interests were all over the place. She thought that French was great, she had a philosophy teacher she was crazy about, and she wanted to do foreign affairs. She was so excited about everything. And when we started to talk to Tom Murnane, the legendary Tufts' development director, about supporting a program, his first thought was the French department because Theresa graduated from a high school in France. He asked us what we thought about it and we responded, "No, we really would like something that involves all departments, all majors." I mean, the whole breadth of Tufts was so exciting to Theresa. We wanted to have something that somehow included all of Tufts. So then it was a question of talking to various people. And I know that as soon as we heard about the R.E.A.L. program, we said: "Hey, that is it."

MR. PRATT: I would add that one of the reasons, at least for me, is that the R.E.A.L. program had the appeal-- quite apart from this other notion that it didn't really single out a particular department—that it gives people a second chance in life because Theresa was a very compassionate and loving person who empathized with the less advantaged. She was going to a very good school herself, but she had plenty of contact with people who hadn't had all the

163

164   Diversity, Resiliency, Legacy

advantages. She always saw the best in people. So, the R.E.A.L. program was attractive for two reasons – one was the nature of the students who were in it in that they almost by definition had some kind of an obstacle or difficulty in the first place; otherwise they would not be resuming their education and would be going up the corporate ladder. And the other reason, at least certainly for me, was that the R.E.A.L. program itself was really one of the kingpins of Tufts. In our view, it seemed like a very specialized, very nice little niche that the big benefactors would easily overlook. So, in a way, the appeal to the underdog, you could almost extend it to the entire program itself. I mean, you talk about 40 to 50 students in a university of 4500 or something like that. Symbolically, the program had the appeal that Theresa would have sympathized with, along with empathizing with the students themselves.

MRS. PRATT: Actually there was one more page to it too. The fact that the R.E.A.L. students were basically day students drawn from the surrounding communities makes it more likely perhaps that they will stay in your communities and work and contribute to these communities. One of the first Pratt scholars told us: "I've gotten my dream job – a juvenile probation officer for Lowell District Court." And we were so tickled that that was her dream job and she had gotten it. The Lowell District Court received a good probation officer. We really like the fact that the local community would benefit also.

Q: You are also actively supporting a special math tutor for the R.E.A.L. students.

MRS. PRATT: Oh yes. They said that was something they have a particular need for.

Q: Why do you think the R.E.A.L. program is important for Tufts University?

MR. PRATT: One thing we should say is that the R.E.A.L. program was in existence long before we arrived on the scene. It brings students on to the campus as full-fledged students, not as special students in a separate program. They are older, more mature, and certainly more worldly-wise. They have experienced something. Something has interrupted their education. In many cases it was financial, but there could be personal, family and all kinds of reasons why these students have taken a detour. So that is one reason. And the other is that they have the potential to give back to the community.

MRS. PRATT: We have a really good English friend who is very observant. And on his first trip to the United States we met him in Arizona and we spent three weeks with him there. We went everywhere, looking at everything, talking to everybody. Once I asked him: "Ray, what surprised you about the United States, what is really going to stick in your mind?" I thought that he would say the Grand Canyon, the dawn or something. And he said: "The one thing that really sticks out in my mind is that in America people get a second chance. In England, by the time you are 25, you have a job, you have a spouse, you have the town you live in. It is not likely that you are going to pull out and do something different. Down here, people are just moving and changing and you don't have to be stuck." And that is part of the R.E.A.L. program.

Q: Do you think it is important to offer people a second chance?

MR. PRATT: Oh, absolutely. But of course in any case the second chance is not a result of their failure. They may need the second chance because of things beyond their own control. It is a process. They go on and do other things until they are ready. That is another reason why the R.E.A.L. program is such an addition to the campus. Many of the students may have gone through various stages and arrive here wiser. They appreciate Tufts and the opportunity perhaps more than some of the other students who come here straight from high school.

You can also see that in the classes, too. Most R.E.A.L. students tend to speak up and participate, present different points of views. They are more mature, more worldly-wise. Somebody once said that education is too precious a thing to waste on the young.

MRS. PRATT: There is a lot of truth to that. Maybe we should have a two or three year gap between high school and college.

MR. PRATT: Compulsory military service or compulsory social service, or get a job. I mean, in a way we have elementary school, middle school, high school, and college. It is all mapped out, and a good case could be made that almost everyone could use an interruption there to have a chance to do something else and appreciate the opportunity of being in college rather than just being told they must go.

Q: I have one more question for you. Where would you like to see the R.E.A.L. program in the future?

166   Diversity, Resiliency, Legacy

MRS. PRATT: Obviously we would like to see it bigger, but that is Tufts' call, not ours. I think it is a wonderful model.

MR. PRATT: I would like to see more scholarship assistance to assure that they could accept all qualified candidates. I would also like to see the R.E.A.L. students to be involved in community service. And some of them would be supporting the R.E.A.L. program themselves one way or another. Through financial gifts or coming and speaking. It is about giving back to society and R.E.A.L. students have the spirit to give back to society. We all know that if you don't have the educational opportunity so many doors are closed to you. So many doors.

MRS. PRATT: I think that Tufts has demonstrated a real commitment to the R.E.A.L. program.

MR. PRATT: President Bacow has certainly been a visible supporter of the program. As we said earlier, one of the reasons we chose to support the R.E.A.L. program, to be honest, is that we saw it as a potentially vulnerable program – a small program in a much bigger place.

Rocco Carzo

Former Director of Athletics
Founder of the Theresa McDermott Carzo Award

Q: I should start by saying that all of my interviews so far have been with R.E.A.L. alumni, so this is actually a great opportunity to speak to somebody from within the university who supports the program and to give us a different perspective on the program and how it has affected them.

A: The pleasure is mine. I would have sought this opportunity out if you hadn't called me. My experience as a faculty member here for 33 years has been nothing but positive. And from that perspective I just couldn't do enough to support the purpose and function of the R.E.A.L. program. It seems to me that it really fulfills the basic premise of an educational institution. And that is to provide opportunities for people who need them but also to provide opportunities beyond what colleges normally do. There are a lot of people out there on the fringes who, through no fault of their own, are hindered in some way from fulfilling their potential.

My wife's case is an unusual one because her father died when she was six years old. She had three sisters and a mother who had to go to work. Each of the sisters graduated from high school and had to go out and support herself. And they are college material. There is no question about that. And my wife was particularly enthusiastic about academic growth, but they all had to put it off. She was lucky that she was here when Tufts instituted this program. It was a great opportunity.

168   Diversity, Resiliency, Legacy

Q: So you were here at Tufts before the program started?

A: I've been here since 1966. The purpose of education is to provide opportunities for people. We hope that if we provide those opportunities for people that they will contribute to society, go out and distinguish themselves and perpetuate this whole idea of helping someone else, reaching out, helping other people to grow by providing opportunities for them. And that is the greatest thing a university can contribute. I went through the same thing. I feel very strongly about it because when I went to school as an athlete on an athletic scholarship, I would never have gone to college without it. And when I got there, there were a lot of people who cared about me, kept an eye on me, kept me in a group that I could identify with.

Q: Did your wife see the uprising R.E.A.L. program as an immediate chance?

A: She was working here on campus at that time in something called the Cedar program. It was a government-sponsored program for people who were underprivileged with personal problems and needed to get themselves into the job market. So, on our campus we taught them typing, I think. The woman who taught them knew my wife and asked her if she would help her. They had classes two or three days a week to help these people who were stuck in the mud or who for some reason had missed out on developing skills to get a reasonable job. And boy, you talk about people appreciating things! Those people used to think that my wife walked on water. She does, of course, but it was nice to see that. And she was doing this when the R.E.A.L. program came up.

Q: You mentioned before we started to have this interview about graduation day for her and what that was like for you being a special part of that.

A: I think her whole experience was inspiring to our entire family. We have four sons and a daughter. Terry had been out of school this long and she got back into the whole educational process with its educational demands. She was a little bit out of sync when she first started because she hadn't been in a formal program of study and had to get back into it. But it didn't take her long to get back in there swinging. She got her rhythm back and then she just jumped right on it while still running a household. I mean that was remarkable. Our kids and myself did everything we could to support her and encourage her because it was a tough haul. Taking full-time classes and running a household too. I wasn't coaching at that time since I was the athletic director in charge of 35 programs instead of just one, so my job was very demanding. But we all pitched in to make it work.

Every time she made progress, we would be all excited. And this whole idea of seeing her graduate and go across the stage was just an awesome experience for all of us. I was the commencement marshal at that time, making sure that all the events went well. It is kind of an unwritten tradition here at Tufts that if a faculty member has a family member who is graduating, we allow them to come up on the stage and present the degree to their family member. So in this case, I had the chance to give it to my wife and give her a big hug up there. And the kids were down there waiting for her. Everybody was clapping. It was a big deal.

Q: That sounds like a wonderful day.

A: It was. And the kids and I, we all talked about how to perpetuate the kind of effort and the kind of example that Terry set about the possibility of resuming your education. So we all chipped in some money and we gave an award in her name. We named it 'The Theresa McDermott Carzo Award.' Each year the award is given to a R.E.A.L. student who made the greatest sacrifice and the greatest progress in their resumed education. They present that every year at the university awards ceremony. My wife goes and hands the award out to the student who wins it. Usually it is two – a male and a female. It is fantastic. There is a plaque now with the names of all the people who have won it.

Q: That is such a wonderful gesture and a great way to carry on the legacy of hard work.

A: I think it is. And we hope that all the people who win the award will pass on their encouragement and enthusiasm to the next generation of R.E.A.L. students.

Q: Do you have a sense of what other faculty members think about the R.E.A.L. program?

A: This is philosophically such a sound program. That is what it is all about, the whole idea of what an education is. In life you can accumulate knowledge. You don't really need to go to college to do that. The question is whether or not that is an education. And no one does this on their own. And that is the key to the whole educational process – putting that wholeness together. It is all about teamwork.

My wife's outlook on all this is that the R.E.A.L. students get more out of the educational process than the students who are straight out of high school. They have been out there, they have worked a little bit, they have a thirst and a hunger

170   Diversity, Resiliency, Legacy

to develop themselves and get a background of knowledge and experience. They want to learn to present themselves and communicate well.

This is what college is all about. College is a place where you not only go to gain knowledge but also it is a place to make mistakes. It is a safe environment. And someone who is resuming their education is very fragile. I mean, you come to school after being out for four or five years and you see all these kids running computers inside out and backwards, and you have to compensate. A whole lot of things pass you by during this period of time that you are out of school. I don't know if there is anything more rewarding than facing those challenges. And it's good for the younger students, too. The world is not only full of seventeen-year-old kids out of high school. You have to interact with people from every dimension and the whole diversity of population is so exciting. And what R.E.A.L. students add to it is age and experience.

Q: Do you think that Tufts is proud enough of its R.E.A.L. alumni? Do you think it does enough to promote the program?

A: That is a tough one to answer. Is Tufts proud of everyone who graduates with a degree? How do they know? How do you know what somebody does for the university? I mean the only way we can help the university is to turn out a product that represents the kind of training and experiences they had at Tufts. One of the things that we should be able to teach them is that you can't do it alone. You need to work with other people and you have to give back. You did not get there on your own. So there is this whole story of going from individual initiative and self-accountability to being able to work with a group. It is really critical because it perpetuates itself. That is what a family is all about. We are as good as the weakest member of our family.

Some are actors, some business leaders, some even become trustees. I am sure that their educational background helped them, the body of knowledge they took away. But I am positive that people helping them and caring for them, interacting with them was even more critical in terms of the educational process. So if we are going to educate this whole person, how do you measure it? I don't know. Who are the biggest givers? Is that a measurement? I know a lot of alumni who come to games and just go up to a kid after a game and say good job. They are passing it on. They are passing on encouragement. I think that is fantastic. So I think to deny what this program does means that you have your eyes closed. You don't really understand it. It's a total educational growth process.

Q: Is there anything else you would like to say about the program?

A: The fact that Tufts recognizes that it is never too late to learn is to me a R.E.A.L. distinction and uniqueness of this university. And that is inspiring.

John Hammock

Professor at Fletcher School of Law and Diplomacy

THE R.E.A.L. PROGRAM: Tufts benefits. The students benefit. The community benefits.

This is what Tufts gets from the program:

- Older students in the classroom with broader and different perspectives. Students who are motivated, who have real life experience and who bring all this to the classroom and to the student body.

- A premier program that shows Tufts is involved in the community and in the civic life of its community. Students who come from diverse cultural and economic backgrounds who participate actively on and off campus and who go on to be global citizens.

- A program that produces ambassadors for Tufts' social commitment and responsibility. The university is taking a leadership role in promoting good citizenship and the civic participation of its students. This program embodies the spirit of this commitment by the university itself—not just by its students.

- A program that provides outreach to minority and disadvantaged communities. This program has brought in people from El Salvador and Haiti; it has opened the door to students in a lower socio-economic status than the typical Tufts student. This diversity enriches Tufts.

174   Diversity, Resiliency, Legacy

- A program that is doing the right thing in an era of cuts of programs for the disadvantaged and those who need a hand. This program illustrates the moral and ethical leadership of this university.

This is what the students get out of the program:

A first class education from a premier university.

A ticket to upward mobility and a job.

An opportunity to become a very grateful member of the Tufts alumni body. R.E.A.L. students more than most are eager to talk about how great Tufts is and to help their alma mater. They are enthusiasts for Tufts.

This is what the community gets out of the program:

Let me explain this through an example. Luis is from El Salvador. I mean from rural El Salvador. I visited his family in their two room home, mud floor, tin roof with chickens and lots of kids running around. This was poor—and I have seen poor throughout the world. Luis left this home, traveled to the United States, worked virtually as an indentured servant, worked his way into a job at MGH and eventually an education at Bunker Hill. He did this through sacrifice, true grit and single mindedness.

As soon as he got his legal papers he applied to the R.E.A.L. program. He was now thirty. No one in his family had even been to high school in El Salvador. None of his Salvadoran buddies in Boston were doing anything except cleaning buildings or washing dishes. He was an outcast. And yet, he finished his degree at Tufts in December. Unlike most of the Salvadorans of his class who are at Tufts cleaning, he now has a Tufts University degree. What does this mean to his community? In El Salvador he went back and gave a talk at the University of Central America; he was on the radio; he participated in a panel of experts at an international forum. Here he was--a peasant from rural El Salvador who was the wrong color and from the wrong background. But he was a Tufts graduate. He was listened to in places he would not have been allowed into just a few years earlier.

What does Luis' story mean for the El Salvador community here in Boston and in the United States? We cannot totally know for he just graduated. But last year he went on the Board of Centro Presente, the leading Central American advocacy group in Boston. He was now accepted as a leader, as a person who stood out and is now ready to have an impact on his community. He is poised to use the chance Tufts gave him to serve his community and his new country.

What Tufts did for Luis has given hope to many that they too can strive to be educated, that they too do not have to clean floors and wash dishes. It has also helped to dispel the notion that immigrants from rural areas cannot do the work, do not have the brain power or the English to make it. Tufts, through Luis, has provided hope to many. And the Tufts image in the immigrant community and in El Salvador is enriched.

Molly Mead

Lincoln-Filene Professor at Tisch College

Q: Could you tell me a little about your experience working with R.E.A.L.
students?

A: I had been teaching for ten years at the University of Massachusetts in
Boston. I taught in the program that was specifically designed for adult
learners. I loved teaching in that program for a few different reasons. One
was that I really saw how adult learners have a sense of purpose about their
education that is just amazing in the classroom. And the second was that I
could see how I could make a difference as a teacher. I could help somebody
who was very motivated to get educated but who also probably lacked some
confidence.

It was very exciting to help someone gain that confidence and understand
oneself as capable of learning. And then I found out that once I could help
someone to get through this, afterwards it was like the sky was the only limit.
It was so exciting. But that school was really designed for adult learners,
students were giving each other support since a lot of the students had kids,
many of them were working part-time if not full-time, they were juggling a
lot of serious responsibilities. Not just the problem of whether or not to have
a beer or do homework.

When I came to Tufts, the first thing I noticed was the overwhelming number
of students who were between 18 and 22. I like to teach them, but I was

178   Diversity, Resiliency, Legacy

missing the basic experience adult learners bring into the classroom. And when I started to learn about the R.E.A.L. program and started to realize that I had a R.E.A.L. student in my class, it was so exciting to kind of pull together things that I had learned from U Mass Boston. The experience and maturity that adult students bring is broadening and can really add to the classroom experience.

For me, one of the things that is important about the R.E.A.L. program is that it creates a peer group of the students; they talk to each other and help each other. "How are you juggling school and a full-time job? How is it feeling to be sitting next to 19 year olds who tend to be faster learners?" I was glad to learn that there is the R.E.A.L. program to offer the students support.

I honestly think that the program should be larger. I just signed the consent form [for this interview] and it seemed that the focus was on the students and the benefit to the students of the R.E.A.L. program, but I want to say that there is a R.E.A.L. benefit to Tufts and to the other students in the classrooms. I would love to see two hundred R.E.A.L. students. I taught a course called "Advocating for Children" and I had two R.E.A.L. students in my class who had had jobs doing child advocacy. They could talk about the experiences in those jobs, whereas the other students were just reading about it. It is so exciting for the teacher to have people who can say: "Well, I actually worked for the department of social services. I worked for the department of transitional systems. Or I worked for a shelter for women and families who are victims of domestic violence. And this is what I have experienced in this area. How does this theory relate to the experience that I had?"

R.E.A.L. students can bring experiential knowledge to the classroom. And their maturity can also rub off on the other students. When students realize that there is a R.E.A.L. student sitting next to them and sometimes realize that this student is struggling to get to class, to do their homework, it causes some of the students to stop and realize: "Wow, I am complaining it is too much reading, but I am sitting next to someone who has a job and kids and she is not complaining about the reading and gets it done."

Q: You have mentioned that a lot of the adult learners lack self-confidence. Where do you think this comes from? A previous educational experience?

A: Yes. Typically for many of the students you could trace it back to elementary school. Some teacher would look at a student and say: "You will never do math. You are hopeless. You will never learn how to write." So, for some of the folks it is a deeply humiliating experience. Maybe the student compensated well enough to go through high school, maybe he or she even started college, but when they are expected to perform to a higher standard, they suddenly remember that the teacher said: "Oh, you will never succeed." And on some level these students internalize it and say to themselves: "Yeah, I have been kind of faking it so far, but now the truth is revealed. I am not that good a student." Also, I think in some cases if you cannot afford to pay for college, it is a little easier to say you were never meant for college anyhow.

Q: To what extent do you think the family plays a role, their family background, relatives not going to college, and so on?

A: If they are the first people in their family to go to college they feel an enormous pride, and on the student's best day, the family is proud of them as well. But in the student's worst moments, the family can drag that person down too. You know, "I didn't go to college, why should you? Things are good enough for me, they should be good enough for you too." Sometimes it even becomes: "Are you trying to show off in some way?" It is also very expensive to go to college, so it takes a bit more sacrifice and also the acceptance of the family. It takes their support. Otherwise they can become an obstacle.

Q: Do you think that colleges, especially high-tiered schools like Tufts, do enough to support adult learners?

A: I think there is a big difference between what public institutions of higher education do to encourage adult learners and the private institutions. Certainly at U Mass Boston there was more encouragement of older students. Here at Tufts, it is much, much less so. I would like to see Tufts increasing the size of the R.E.A.L. program and basically say: "We believe in Tufts' education, we think it is a fantastic education and more people should have the opportunity to benefit from this education. More adult learners should have the opportunity. We think that our institution would be more diverse if we had more adult learners."

Robert Fera

Professor of Psychology, Middlesex Community College
Tufts Alumnus

Q: Please tell me about your relationship with the R.E.A.L. program.

A: I became aware of the R.E.A.L. program when I started working at Middlesex Community College almost 25 years ago. I was a counselor in the center where we do the personal transfer counseling that involves helping students to leave Middlesex and go to a four-year school. At that point we already had some students transferring into the R.E.A.L. program. I was in the counseling center for a few years and then started to teach. I had a position as a department chair and professor. Then I actually saw students in the classroom who were doing well and with whom I would talk about the program.

Q: Were you looking for a certain student with specific characteristics?

A: Sure. Since I received my master's degree from Tufts, I had some knowledge of Tufts and the R.E.A.L. program. And certainly I would look for someone who wrote well and had really strong verbal skills. That was really important. Also being comfortable in class in terms of leading discussions. I was looking for people who were confident or were beginning to be confident in their academic skills.

182   Diversity, Resiliency, Legacy

Q: What are the common obstacles for students coming from the community college?

A: The biggest obstacle is the course load itself. Obviously more reading would be required, more writing, just more work in general. So they go from doing really, really well where they excelled at Middlesex, to entering a totally different league. Then there is the economic divide. I went to the showing of a documentary about Michelle Botus. She is a current R.E.A.L. student. She is a single mom with four kids. She went through poverty, domestic abuse, and homelessness and it is a really extreme and phenomenal achievement for her to be graduating from Tufts.

And finally you work through all that and you still have a couple of obstacles. One of them is the psychological perspective, whether or not they can see themselves at Tufts. A community college, yeah. But Tufts University? That is really not in the cards for me, it is for someone else. They have to get through the psychological barrier.

One of the privileges I had was to work with some of the students who overcame so many barriers. I had students who lived out of their car. Just amazing. Actually one of the first students I knew who came to Tufts was Kirk. He was homeless and he had been dependent on substances. He had burned all the bridges that he had. Then he entered a substance abuse treatment facility, and came to Middlesex. We were happy to have him in the program and in classes. He is just an amazing guy. And slowly and surely, we worked on his recovery. He excelled. He is an incredibly bright guy. He was the commencement speaker at Middlesex. This was 15 to 20 years ago. Faculty members and many other people were crying. It was incredibly emotional.

He told the story of being homeless and how he would look up this hill at Tufts when he was drunk and in the end he said: "And now, I will tell you that I will be going to Tufts in the fall." He came to Tufts and did really well, graduated and for many years worked with people with substance abuse and other issues. And with every person I know, it is a different story. But it is also similar in terms of the obstacles and struggles, psychological, economic, social, and logistical, virtually all of them have multiple layers of obstacles. They come to Middlesex first, they are able to excel and then make it successfully through Tufts.

Q: What do you think it is that the R.E.A.L. program offers them?

A: I think that it offers them many things. First of all, it offers them an entrée to Tufts University. Tufts is a really great school. It is one of the most wonderful schools in the country. And for anyone to be able to come here, I mean when I came here, I was from a working class family and I felt like: "Oh my god, I am very lucky to be here in the graduate program." And so I think that these students have the same sense of awe, confirmation and affirmation about themselves. I think that it takes them into a whole different world most of them haven't even been aware of.

The R.E.A.L. program offers them the support to be successful in this new environment. So that if there is one thing, I am of course biased, I wish there would be more R.E.A.L. students admitted, because if there would be a greater diversity in the program with a larger number of students, the better off they would be because they would have even more of a support system.

Q: Do you think that the R.E.A.L. students bring something different from the regular undergraduates to the campus? And if yes, what is it?

A: There is a very substantial trend in psychology, positive psychology, towards resilience, which I am very interested in. And many of these students like Michelle, like you, like all the other students I have had in class or counseling who bring a legacy of resilience with them, they bring these American stories, the American Dream, you know, the from rags to riches story. Some of these students were tremendously underprivileged. If you would twist the events just a bit the other way, they could be in jail, could be in a psychiatric institution, could be at home watching television on welfare, but through a number of factors, but particularly through their resilience, their perseverance, they find a way to get through any of the obstacles. They have achieved, and have achieved at a very high level.

Robert Hollister

Dean of Tisch College

Q: Dean Hollister, please tell me about your experience with the R.E.A.L. program.

A: I have had students from the R.E.A.L. program in classes that I taught and I have also had informal interactions with R.E.A.L. students. On occasion I have gone to the annual luncheon for faculty and administrators involved with the program.

The students in my classes did good work academically and they added significantly to the quality of classroom discussions because they had additional life experience that elevated and enhanced the discussions. I think that was the primary thing.

I am not teaching now so my interactions are more informal. They include occasional contact with R.E.A.L. students who participate in the Tisch College activities. One is Michelle Botus. I met her prior to her coming to Tufts. We were on a panel together about homelessness in Massachusetts. Also, the Tisch College sponsors a class called 'Producing TV Shows for Social Change.' The class consists of a group of students producing a short documentary. Last year one of those student films was about family homelessness and it featured Michelle and her family. It was an account of her experience as a formerly homeless woman. It was a very powerful experience. Michelle was eloquent and inspiring in her participation in the public screening at the end of the

186 Diversity, Resiliency, Legacy

term. She is just another example of the way in which the life experience of R.E.A.L. students contributes in significant ways to the education of other students at Tufts, both undergraduate and graduate.

Another student, Tina Johnson, has been a valued member of our staff here. And there is Anne Stevenson who is a political science major, very active in the Democratic Party. She has worked closely with two of our senior fellows, Alan Salomont and Tom Birmingham. And again, I have been impressed with her energy, insights and initiative.

Q: How well do you think the R.E.A.L. program fits the Tufts philosophy?

A: I think it is a perfect fit. Tufts has a deep tradition of open access to higher education. I have always felt that the R.E.A.L. program was an important expression of that broad principle. And certainly the current leadership of Tufts and President Bacow, who is a compelling advocate of need-blind admission, promote an institutional commitment to removing barriers to access.

I would also like to mention that the mission of the Tisch College is to prepare students for a lifetime of active citizenship. Our mission is consistent with that of Tufts in promoting democratic principles and the R.E.A.L. program has successfully contributed to a broader representation of the population in the student body. In order to be a fully democratic institution, we need to attract and support a diverse student body. Diversity in its multiple dimensions includes age and life experience, as well as racial background. Also, a successfully diverse student body can result in a higher quality of education for everybody. So the theme of diversity gives another key rationale for the R.E.A.L. program.

Q: What do you think Tufts should do to have a more diverse student body?

A: The main thing is to raise more financial aid. I haven't looked at the statistics recently but the proportion of the students who get no financial aid is well over half. I am very pleased that the top priority within the current Tufts capital campaign is to increase undergraduate financial aid. I think it is consistent with Tufts' philosophy--including the R.E.A.L. program--to making a contribution to this area in terms of social purpose.

Q: Do you think that the R.E.A.L. program is large enough within the university to actually make an impact?

A: That is a really good question. I would love the program to be a bit larger. I think it would take additional money to accomplish that. My advocacy would be to sustain the program in its current size and provide it with a stable financial base first. As a longer term goal increasing the size of the program would be very desirable. You could make a good argument that approximately forty students is not a sufficient critical mass. However, it is certainly better than if the program did not exist.

Q: Where would you like to see the program in the future?

A: I would like to see it at least as large as it is today. And I would like to see it fully endowed with that level of stability. I would also advocate for more visibility of the program internally and externally. This project that you are making now can be a contribution to that. Also, the other regular communication vehicles on campus might help. I am impressed, for example, with the number of faculty who know about the program. Maybe there is some way that the faculty's support could be reinforced. Or just be more creative, like the documentary about Michelle. She had a profound impact on the couple hundred undergraduates who saw the film. It would also be a positive thing if a few more trustees of the university were champions of the program. To find a way that the governing board of the university could be fully supportive of the program is an important part of the puzzle.

Q: You have mentioned that you were surprised by the number of faculty who were knowledgeable about the program. Do you have any kind of feedback from the professors about the program and its students?

A: What I pick up informally from my faculty colleagues is that they are glad that the program exists; they have had positive experiences with the R.E.A.L. students in their classes. Another thing is that a lot of faculty have concern that much of the undergraduate population comes from a background of amazing privilege and there is a strong interest in having an impact on a broader group of people. Because that is their value system, wanting their teaching impact to be something more than just to help privileged people do well in life.

Barbara Rubel

Director of Community Relations

It seems that the R.E.A.L. program has been at Tufts as long as I can remember. I first learned about the program in the 1970s, not long after I arrived at Tufts. My first interaction with the program was over a space issue. The lounge space R.E.A.L. was using was coveted by another student organization, and somehow I was drawn into the discussion. I learned some of the stories of the R.E.A.L. students at that time and was amazed at their persistence and resourcefulness as they not only worked hard in the classroom, but found ways to juggle the logistics of their lives in order to get to the campus every day. As a young, single woman who never questioned my right to go to college and even graduate school, this made a deep impression on me.

I next remember the experience of paying attention to the applicants to Tufts from our host communities of Medford and Somerville, and doing what I could to encourage their admission in order to increase the presence on campus of local residents, which many of the R.E.A.L. students are.

My most recent encounter with R.E.A.L. was a chance meeting with a new R.E.A.L. student. She and I happened to be in a Davis Square store at the same time and struck up a conversation. When she mentioned that she would be starting at Tufts in the fall and that she would be studying geology I guessed that she was transferring. I was pleased to hear that she was coming in through the R.E.A.L. program, and delighted to know that it was still going strong. This student began to glow as she described her fears that she had lost the opportunity to get a college degree from a university like Tufts. She expressed genuine gratitude at the opportunity that was being

190   Diversity, Resiliency, Legacy

extended to her, amazement at the support that was offered and the way she was welcomed here.

R.E.A.L. tends to keep a low profile on campus and is not advertised loudly to off-campus constituents. In fact, when I mention R.E.A.L. to people in Medford and Somerville, they are often hearing about the program for the first time. The response is most often surprise and satisfaction. For residents of Medford and Somerville, Tufts often seems unattainable and elitist. For some neighbors of the campus, their most significant interaction with Tufts students is not a pleasant one. It may occur at 3 a.m. when neighbors want to sleep and students are still enjoying themselves. It's very important to the university for those neighbors and many others to know that Tufts is about more than undergrads looking for a party.

When they hear about the R.E.A.L. program and the opportunity it presents to people who have had to deal with challenges but are pursuing a college degree no matter what, and have been welcomed and supported to come to Tufts, it changes the whole tone of the conversation. The R.E.A.L. program represents, in many ways, the best of what Tufts is all about. We are helping people study, expand their worlds, and arm themselves to make far more significant contributions to society than they otherwise would. The R.E.A.L. program is one of the aspects of Tufts of which I'm most proud.

Breinigsville, PA USA
07 December 2009
228793BV00001B/4/P